Understanding Crime

Why we took the wrong road in the war against crime

E.W. Chandler, B.S., J.D., LL.M

ISBN 978-1798936122

Front cover image: "The Fall and Expulsion from Garden of Eden," Michelangelo, 1509-1510. Fresco, Sistine Chapel, Vatican.

Back cover photo from the author's archives.

Interior graphics referenced at their locations.

First printing 2019.

Layout and design by
Wind Song Press
windsong@mtnhome.com

Published in the United States by
A to Z Publishing Group
www.atozpublishinggroup.com

Please direct inquiries to:
Edward Witt Chandler
wittdaux@gmail.com

Dedication

To my children—Laura, Heather, Elizabeth, and Forrest—who have taught me so much. From them I have learned to love, to forgive, and to appreciate life in all of its variety.

Also, to my wife Laura Phillips, who has been an incomparable inspiration to me. Her way of thinking, and even the arguments we've had, have contributed to my life and pursuit of education in ways that have moved me to critically think and write with heart.

The completion of this book was very important to me. I am grateful to my family for helping to make this possible.

Table of Contents

THE APPENDIX TO THIS BOOK may be downloaded from www.edwardwittchandler.com free of charge. References to Appendix pages in this book will appear in brackets in this form: [Appendix, p.   ].

About the Author

Photo from *The Jackson Sun*, Benton County, Tennessee, 1980. The author (left), shown with a client accused of killing his girlfriend by shooting her in the face, first-degree murder. The client was found guilty and sentenced to life, avoiding the death penalty—defense: insanity and intoxication, psychotic due to drug abuse, meth, and PCP. This case became a turning point in Chandler's life as a defense lawyer, after which he became intensely interested in crime and biology.

EDWARD WITT CHANDLER is a retired Tennessee criminal defense lawyer who now lives in the Ozark Mountains of Arkansas. In the late 1960s, he was one of the first three full-time public defenders in Shelby County, Tennessee. He was a criminal defense lawyer in the trenches of the war against crime for over 40 years.

Chandler holds a B.S. from Bethel College 1963 and is a graduate of Vanderbilt University 1967 (J.D.) and the University of Washington 1978 (LL.M.). He completed his military obligation in the U.S. Marine Corps. He was also an assistant professor of criminal justice, University of

Memphis 1976-1977, and an adjunct member of the faculty for several years. He has been a lecturer at continuing legal education seminars for lawyers in Tennessee, Arkansas, Missouri, and Texas.

On November 13, 1985, Chandler presented a paper entitled "Cloning Criminals: The Death of the Doctrine of Free Will," to the American Society of Criminology's 37th Annual Meeting in San Diego, California. His articles include "A Crime Free Society: Genetic Engineering: Will It Be a Viable Solution to Curb our Nation's Rising Crime Problem?" (*Memphis Press-Scimitar,* October 3, 1983) [Appendix, p. 40]; "A Criminal-Free Society Through Gene Splicing" (*The Commercial Appeal*, March 31, 1985) [Appendix, p. 41]; "Sex, Death and Lawyer's Ethics" (*ATLA Docket*, June 1998) [Appendix, pp. 48-53]; and "The Genetic Defect Defense" (*ATLA Docket*, Arkansas Trial Lawyers Association, Spring 1999) [Appendix, pp. 56-61].

TO THE READER: If I have used words, paragraphs, or ideas in this book without reference to their source, this would only be because the information I have collected spans many years of study, and some reference notes may have been lost in the shuffle. Every attempt has been made to reference the many books and ideas I have encountered over the years. Any conclusions and opinions I have expressed in this book are my own, and not necessarily attributed to the authors I have referenced. I hope that the sources I have used will inspire readers to embark on research of their own. Many of the books and articles I am using in this book are still relevant, inspirational, and available. — Edward Witt Chandler

Foreword

Don't believe everything you think.

— Allan Lokos

THE PAINTING on the cover of this book is the biblical Garden of Eden as depicted by Michelangelo's 16th-century fresco on the ceiling of the Vatican's Sistine Chapel. Adam and Eve are tempted by the serpent to eat the fruit from the tree of knowledge of good and evil.

According to ancient Jewish and Christian scholars, "free will" was born in the Garden of Eden with the fall of man. Criminal responsibility under English common law was based upon that "free will which God hath given to man" and became law in the colonies and the states and the federal government. But is "free will" instead an illusion—and the Garden of Eden a biblical myth? Or, cringing with shame, were Adam and Eve actually expelled from the Garden for disobeying?

The biblical fall of Adam and Eve, including their expulsion from the Garden of Eden, was adopted by three great monotheistic religions: Judaism, Christianity, and Islam, although the view of Islam in the Quran differs slightly. Eden is called "Jannah" (the garden). It is regarded as a physical place and also a spiritual realm. The Quran also describes only one tree in the garden (Quran 2:35).

Women's creation from man's "side" or "rib" stimulates cross-cultural and anthropological observations. Genesis may have been influenced by, or serve as a response to, the Sumerian Dilmun (paradise) myth. This myth recounts how the god Enki is cursed by the goddess Ninhursag because he ate plants she bore painlessly. Ninhursag then creates the goddess Nin-Ti ("lady of the rib" or "lady who makes live") to heal his broken body. Adam may be seen as "giving birth" to Eve, as Dionysus is born from Zeus's thigh and Athena, from his head.

In the story, contrary to popular belief, it is not woman who tempts man, but the snake and the tree itself that tempt woman. God had forbidden earthlings to eat from the tree. In her response to the snake, the woman adds, "But God said, 'Neither shall you touch it, lest you die.'" God informs the humans, "Of the tree of the knowledge of good and evil you shall not eat, for in the day you eat from it you will surely die." This verse prompts theological questions: Is God tempting the humans? Does the Deity know what will happen? Has the Deity planned the "fall"? Was humanity originally mortal or immortal?

After explaining evolution in *On the Origin of the Species by Means of Natural Selection* (1859), Charles Darwin (1809-1892) examined the evolution of humans in his book *The Descent of Man and Selection Related to Sex* (1871) and disputed Biblical creation. His idea was that humans belong to a species descended from a common ancestor shared with other animals.

Scientific American published an article titled "First of Our Kind: Could *Australopithecus sediba* Be Our Long Lost Ancestor?" by Kate Wong, who said:

Sometime between three million and two million years ago, perhaps on a primeval savanna in Africa, our ancestors became recognizably human. For more than a million years their australopithecine predecessors— Lucy and her kind, who walked upright like us yet still possessed the stubby legs, tree-climbing hands and small brains of their ape forebears—had thrived in and around the continent's forests and woodlands. But their world was changing. Shifting climate favored the spread of open grasslands, and the early australopithecines gave rise to new lineages. One of these offshoots evolved long legs, toolmaking hands and an enormous brain. This was our genus, *Homo*, the primate that would rule the planet. (April 2012)

Did humans evolve from a single woman (mitochondrial Eve) or from a small group of women who lived about 200,000 years ago in Africa? Not all scientists support this hypothesis. The fact of evolution (descent with modification from lower to higher forms of life over billions of years) must be distinguished from the theory of evolution or human understanding of precisely how evolution occurs.

The fact of evolution is as scientifically well-established as the fact that the moon orbits the earth. *Newsweek's* cover of January 11, 1988, carried the full story of "Mitochondrial Eve" to the world [Appendix p. 76]. However, many aspects of the theory of evolution are still under debate today.

The fact that the moon orbits the earth has been known since ancient times. The Greeks, Romans, and Egyptians knew it. Empirical rules for how it does so emerge with Kepler. A true quantitative theory of how and why it does so had to await the genius of Newton's law of universal gravitation. A fundamental understanding of the workings of gravity itself had to await Einstein's general theory of relativity. The understanding of crime is yet to come.

In the first centuries after Christ, Christians read and followed a variety of scripture. Christians held beliefs that today would be considered bizarre. Some believed that there were two, twelve, or as many as thirty gods. Some thought that a malicious deity, rather than the true God, created the world. Some maintained that Christ's death and resurrection had nothing to do with salvation, while others insisted that Christ never died. In the Middle Ages and the Renaissance, the religious wars of the sixteenth century were replete with Christians murdering Christians, witch trials, and other atrocities.

A 2005 Harris Poll found that 63 percent of liberals but only 37 percent of conservatives believed that humans and apes have a common ancestry (Shermer, 2006). According to a 2013 Pew Research Center poll ("Public's views"), only 33 percent of all adults surveyed believed that living beings have always existed in their present form, broken down as follows: 64 percent of white evangelical Christians, 50 percent of black Protestants, 31 percent of Hispanic Catholics, 26 percent of white Catholics, 20 percent of those unaffiliated with a church, and 15 percent of white mainline Protestants. Politically, 48 percent of Republicans were creationists, compared with 27 percent of Democrats and 28 percent of Independents.

What these figures confirm for us is that there are religious and political reasons for rejecting evolution. But as a matter of fact, we evolved.

Near the end of the play *Inherit the Wind* by Jerome Lawrence and Robert E. Lee, which debuted in 1955 and is based on the famous 1920s trial of John Scopes in Dayton, Tennessee, the girlfriend of a man who's been charged with teaching Darwinian evolution says:

> I haven't really thought very much. I was always afraid of what I might think—so it seemed safer not to think at all. But now I know. A thought is like a child inside our body. It has to be born. If it dies inside you, part of you dies, too. Maybe what Mr. Darwin wrote is bad. I don't know. Bad or good, it doesn't make any difference. The ideas have to come out—like children. Some of 'em healthy as a bean plant, some sickly. I think the sickly ideas die mostly, don't you, Bert?

I do not argue that God does not exist, or that the Bible is not the word of God, or that Jesus did not die on the cross. My question: Is the Garden of Eden a myth? If so, civilization took the wrong road in its method to prevent and control crime.

I

Introduction

And out of the ground
made the Lord God
to grow every tree
that is pleasant to the sight,
and good for food;
the tree of life also
in the midst of the garden,
and the tree of knowledge
of good and evil.

— Genesis 2:9

IF YOU BELIEVE there was an Adam and Eve, and that there was a Garden of Eden as depicted in the Bible, you will most likely not understand my argument about the cause of crime. I submit, instead, humans evolved from creatures in the sea. Charles Darwin's scientific theory of evolution as outlined in his book *On the Origin of Species by Means of Natural Selection,* printed in London by John Murray in 1859, is the backbone of my argument: Humans are animals. Humans are mammals. We evolved. To understand human behavior, look to biology and evolution—not the Bible.

> *I do not feel obliged to believe that the same God who has endowed us with senses, reason, and intellect has intended us to forgo their use.*
>
> — *Galileo Galilei*

In the late 1970s, I read a book called *The First Three Minutes*, published in 1977 by Steven Weinberg, who went on to receive the 1979 Nobel Prize in physics. The website of the University of Texas, Austin, lists Steven as the Jack S. Josey-Welch Foundation Chair in Science and Regental Professor, as well as Director, Theory Research Group. I found his book fascinating. My mind was opened. I began to think about crime in terms of evolution and the 14 billion years since the "Big Bang." I now see a much different picture than my grandmother's Adam and Eve in the Garden of Eden.

Later in the 1970s, I attended a course at the University of California, Los Angeles, and heard a series of lectures by world-famous astrophysicists. Again, fascinating. I was working in contract administration for Hughes Aircraft, Los Angeles, and I was interested in the origin and structure of our universe and who we were for many different reasons.

On a remote island in the Canadian Arctic wilderness, scientists recently found the remains of a 375-million-year-old fossil fish (*Tiktaalik roseae*) that crawled on land. Complex bodily changes occurred when this distant ancestor of ours moved out of the water. It was

a strange creature, a combination of the limbs, skull, neck, and ribs of four-limbed animals, and the more primitive jaw, fins, and scales of fish. It seems to be an intermediate step between fish and land-living animals, a key link in the evolutionary chain that led to amphibians, reptiles, and dinosaurs.

Researchers had conducted five annual fossil-hunting expeditions to Canada's Ellesmere Island, 830 miles south of the North Pole, before they hit pay dirt.... One afternoon a member of the team spotted what looked like the snout of a flat-headed fish sticking out of a cliff.

"We figured we'd find the rest of the skeleton inside the mountain, which is exactly what happened," says Neil H. Shubin, a team co-leader at the University of Chicago....[1]

The newly discovered fossil fish was a predator that could reach nine feet in length. It lived in shallow freshwater but was able, researchers believe, to pull itself out of the water and move around on land. (The name *Tiktaalik* means "large freshwater fish" in Inuktitut.) In the late Devonian period, nearly 400 million years ago, the area where the fossils were found was near the equator and had the temperature and climate of the Amazonian rainforest. As the Earth's continental plates shifted, the land drifted north to the Canadian Arctic. (Marsa, 2009)

Later, when the most recent glacial epoch peaked, 18,000 years ago, the earth of our ancestors had continental ice a mile thick as far south as the Great Lakes. Lower sea-surface temperatures and an atmosphere averaging four to six degrees Celsius colder than ours today shaped a global climate both more and less hospitable. A vegetation model applied to an Ice Age climate model indicates patterns of vegetation in which some desert areas are wetter than at present, tropical rainforests are smaller and in different locations, and temperate and subtropical forests and woodlands are more widespread. Tundra and high-latitude forests occur much farther south in the Northern Hemisphere and even claim the southern end of South America.

An analysis of *Tiktaalik's* anatomy...indicates that the evolution of fins into sturdy limbs was accompanied by

---

1 "Neil Shubin, a professor at the University of Chicago, was a student of [Farish] Jenkins at Harvard and would go on to spend 30 years in the field with his mentor and friend. Shubin was with Jenkins on Ellesmere Island in Nunavut Territory, Canada, when they discovered Tiktaalik roseae." Read more about Farish Jenkins on p. 9 of this book.

other anatomical innovations, including the rudiments of an articulated neck. "What allowed this lineage of animals to start to exploit the land was not just a matter of changing the fins to limbs but also the ability to move their head so they could navigate in shallow water," says Ted Daeschler, a team coleader and a paleontologist at the Academy of Natural Sciences in Philadelphia. (Marsa, 2009)

In *Your Inner Fish* (2009), Neil Shubin takes us on a 3.5 billion year journey into the history of the human body. As one of the discoverers of *Tiktaalik*, he says on page 27, "Seeing Lucy we can understand our history as highly advanced primates. Seeing *Tiktaalik* is seeing our history as fish."

II

The Beginning

*Knowledge is of two kinds. We know a subject
ourselves, or we know where we can find information
upon it.*

— Samuel Johnson

FOR BILLIONS OF YEARS, a primordial rock circled our solar system between Mars and Jupiter.[2] Then, 65 million years ago, some unknown celestial mechanics pushed this 9-mile-wide projectile out of its orbit and it struck Earth, traveling 45,000 miles per hour. It hit in the Gulf of Mexico off Mexico's Yucatan peninsula and excavated a hole 20 miles deep. Air surged at speeds exceeding 600 mph, bringing hurricane-force winds to what is now North America. An explosion of heat reaching more than 36,000 degrees Fahrenheit spread from this impact site.

Vegetation vaporized. A debris plume erupted above Earth's atmosphere and rained down around the globe, creating regional infernos. This was just the beginning. A blanket of chemicals covered the Earth and fell as acid rain. Photosynthesis nearly stopped. Forests died. Wildfires turned the surface of the earth to soot now found all over the earth.

---

2 "Astronomers have long suspected that our solar system coalesced from a vast cloud of gas and dust" (Fox, 2019). The formation of our solar system was a messy, chaotic process that ejected all kinds of bodies out to the far fringes. Today there are four giant outer planets in our solar system. There may be at least a fifth to be discovered. The Large Synoptic Survey Telescope (LSST) under construction atop Cerro Pachon in Chile will scan the sky, and eventually, it should discover hundreds or even thousands of bodies on the fringe. We do not even know how many planets are in our solar system. It's a mystery. Some may be 100 billion miles away. (See Powell, 2016)

Tiny plankton and large dinosaurs froze or starved. Nothing on land larger than 55 pounds survived. Most damaging was the sulfur and the dust. A world-wide layer of iridium (common in asteroids but not on earth) covered the earth.

This was the most important natural event that had occurred in the last 100 million years. According to the fossil record, approximately 75 percent of all species were lost. So far, scientists have determined there have been five mass extinctions. This was the fifth and most recent. If you're interested in the topic of mass extinctions, Dr. Viviane Richter, whose background is in structural biology, has summarized them in an article in *Cosmos: The Science of Everything* called "The Five Big Mass Extinctions."

The impact scar of this event is called Chicxhlub (pronounced CHICK-soo-loob), after a nearby town. The size of the Chicxhlub crater was 112 to 114 miles in diameter. As the asteroid killed 75 percent of life on earth and ended the 180-million-year reign of the dinosaurs and left its mark in Mexico, the earth burned. Some spores and seeds survived the fires. Some avian dinosaurs died; others lived. Some of the birdlike creatures or species that survived became our modern birds. They had beaks without teeth, ideal for seeds. Carnivorous species died as their food sources, but dinosaurs with toothless beaks could feast on fallen seeds long after the plants died. And other forms of life emerged from the ash. Mammals soon flourished.

Fossil discoveries have illustrated evolutionary transitions from fish to four-legged animals, from dinosaurs to birds, from reptiles to mammals, from land-dwelling mammals to whales and sea cows, from limbed reptiles to snakes, from apes to man. Humans evolved. Humans, whose ancestors were mammals who survived the damage caused by that catastrophic event 65 million years ago, became cavemen. Birds are descendants of dinosaurs, and we are descendants of a small mammal.

Neanderthals have been extinct for 40,000 years, but *Homo sapiens* interbred with Neanderthals and Denisovans[3] between fifty and sixty thousand years ago. DNA studies of ancient DNA of both subspecies indicate that around one to four percent of the genome of modern humans comes from these ancient hominins. Neanderthal-inherited genes make modern people slightly more prone to depression, nicotine addiction, allergies, and clotting disorders. However, this was a modest contribution to these traits for some populations.

The following excerpt is from an article by Zach Zorich, published in *Archaeology Magazine*: "Timelines: Tracking when humans, Neanderthals, and Denisovans crossed paths—and what became of their offspring":

> The earliest hominins that are part of the genus *Homo* evolved in Africa at least 2.2 million years ago. Some of them, early members of the species *Homo erectus*, left the continent around 2 million years ago. Over time, hominins in different places began to evolve into separate species and subspecies. Neanderthals became a distinct group in Europe around 250,000 years ago, *Homo sapiens* continued to evolve in Africa, and Denisovans probably arose from what may have been a group of Neanderthals isolated in Asia. The prevailing wisdom has been that *Homo sapiens*...and Neanderthals didn't interbreed until around 50,000 or 60,000 years ago, according to genetic research. At some point, as modern humans spread through Asia, they encountered and interbred

---

3 Denisovans are extinct hominins (closely related to extinct Neanderthals). In 2010, scientists confirmed the existence of these hominins in Siberia in Denisovan Cave. (Alex, 2016) [Appendix p. 74-75.

with Denisovans there as well. The evidence of this interbreeding appears in our genome—but not in that of Neanderthals who lived in Europe and the Middle East or in that of Denisovans—which suggests that the hybrid offspring of interbreeding of those interbreeding events became part of the *Homo sapiens* population. (July/August, 2016)

In 2015, it was announced that human fossils had been discovered underground in a cave called Rising Star near Johannesburg, South Africa. The bones belonged to a new species that was named *Homo naledi*. These remains were dated to between 236,000 and 350,000 years old. Scientists maintain that *Homo naledi's* primitive features link to much earlier members of the human family, and that this species might even be a direct ancestor of ours (*Homo sapiens*). *Homo naledi* lived at a time when human ancestors were making sophisticated stone tools in the Middle Stone Age tradition (Wong, 2017).

From Permian to Triassic (251 million years ago)

The third of the five mass extinctions, when almost all life on earth (96 percent, according to Dr. Richter) had been extinguished by volcanoes, marked the end of the Permian Period and began the Triassic. Most of the giant amphibians and reptiles had died out, but turtles, lizards, frogs, crocodiles, dinosaurs, and mammals got their start during this era.

Greenland has furnished tiny teeth and jaws of mammals of our ancestors. Their skulls had a simplified hinge joint that worked with enlarged jaw-closing muscles to both strengthen and fine-tune chewing movements. Cusps on their teeth made chewing more efficient. Their baby teeth were replaced by adult teeth. These fossils were discovered in frozen rocks in the 1990s by Farish Jenkins, a Harvard University paleontologist (and U.S. Marine) who always had a rifle with him to protect his arctic team from polar bears. Farish and Neil Shubin, his student, were part of the team that discovered *Tiktaalik,* as described on page 3

This is a signature feature of mammal biology. Babies without teeth or with baby teeth can nurse their mother's milk, which is produced by the mammary glands that give mammals their name. This allowed the mammals to grow faster, survive better, and have a higher metabolism that allowed the early forms to be active in colder environments, especially in the darkness of night.

These early mammals also had huge brains compared with their ancestors, though not as enormous as modern mammal brains. They had large olfactory bulbs and auditory regions, with keen senses of smells and hearing, as well as brain regions that processed tactile input from skin and brain.

But their tiny Triassic stem mammalia forms were not the dominant animals of their day. That distinction belonged to dinosaurs and crocodiles. They were at the top of the food chain. Proto-mammals such as the morganucodans did have strong jaws, however, to crush large insects. Kuehneotheriids ate soft worms or moths with delicate teeth. Haramiyidans ate small plants. They had uniquely small jaws.

From Triassic to Jurassic (200 million years ago)

About 200 million years ago, the Triassic period ended and the Jurassic period began. The supercontinent Pangaea tore apart. Volcanoes poisoned the atmosphere. Catastrophe struck. But some mammals somehow survived, and some dinosaurs survived this fourth mass extinction.

Scientists have found fossils in northeastern China of different forms from 30 million years after this mass extinction. My favorite: Castorocauda, a creature the size of a prairie dog with webbed hands and feet and a flattened tail like a beaver—the earliest known swimming mammal. Some other types burrowed underground. Others climbed trees. Another looked like a flying squirrel gliding through branches, riding air currents. Outside of China, in Colorado, scientists describe an ant-eating digger. Eventually, the mammal family tree contained the "egg layers" and the therians (marsupials and placentals) [Appendix, pp. 30-31].

They were few and they were small, but the repenomamus were wolverine-sized creatures who lived from the mid-Jurassic period through the Cretaceous Period of China where fossilized stomach contents included the bones of small dinosaurs. But these dinosaur-eaters went into decline and barely made it out of the Cretaceous Period.

Painting by James Gurney, from the article "The Ascent of Mammals" by S. Brusatte and Z. Luo, *Scientific American*, June 2016, p. 29. "DINO for dinner: A roughly 130-million-year-old fossil of early mammal *Repenomamus* from China was found with the bones of a baby psittacosaur in its rib cage."

In 1824, British naturalist William Buckland announced he had found fossils of an ancient lizard-like animal he called

Megalosaurus,[4] as well as tiny mammal jaws and cusped teeth alongside it. They were about the size of the jaws of today's mouse. These fossils dated to the Middle Jurassic period. Mammals were not, in evolution, a recent creature as scholars had believed.

But why did some mammals (placentals) rise to dominance? Today there are 6,400 recognized species of animals, from bats to whales, that cover the planet (Burgin, Colella, Kahn, & Upham, 2018). Humans are the number one animal killer. We are the dominant vertebrae creature.

The demise of the dinosaur and other creatures allowed placental mammals to survive. Mammals by definition include egg-laying monotremes, the marsupials (who raise babies in pouches), and placentals, as well as all the extinct descendants of their common ancestor Today's mammals evolved from *cynodonts*, a primitive species that had reptilian features [Appendix, pp. 30-31].

From Jurassic to Cretaceous (145 million years ago)

By the beginning of the Cretaceous period, 145 million years ago, the modern mammal blueprint was established. Big brains and fast growth rates were key traits. And a minor evolutionary change became a game changer: tribosphenic molars. A projection on the upper molar fits into a basin on the corresponding lower molar and the two work together to crunch food like a mortar and pestle. This tooth arrangement opened a door of new dietary possibilities. Armed with tribosphenic teeth, therians began to diversify. The eutherians (that evolved into placentals) and metatherians (that later became marsupials) split.

In the lower Cretaceous period, 125 million years ago, a new type of plant evolved: angiosperm ("seed in a vessel"). The flower- and fruit-bearing shrub and tree that

---

4 Megalosaurus ("great lizard") was the first dinosaur to be named.

make up most of today's plant species also provides many of our dietary staples and decorates our gardens. Angiosperms colonized landscapes around the world. Mammals had a new source of food: fruits and flowers and the insects that fed on them. The tribosphenic molar (of therians) was the perfect tool for processing this new food, and so they proliferated. Mammals with more primitive dentitions (e.g. repenomamus) perished. In their article "The Ascent of Mammals," Stephen Brusatte (a paleontologist at the University of Edinburgh in Scotland) and Zhe-Xi Luo (a paleontologist at the University of Chicago) wrote:

> While therians were feasting on bugs during the middle and later parts of the Cretaceous, some other, more primitive mammal groups evolved complex dentitions that were well suited to slicing and grinding the new angiosperms. The northern continents became overrun by multituberculates—bucktoothed vermin that looked like rats. Despite appearances, these creatures were not closely related to true rodents but rather converged on a rodentlike body plan because they were eating similar foods. Recent studies by Gregory Wilson of the University of Washington and David M. Grossnickle of the University of Chicago have applied sophisticated statistical analysis to big databases of fossil measurements to show that multituberculates were thriving in the latest part of the Cretaceous. They were evolving into many species, growing to ever larger sizes and developing more intricate molars in a coevolutionary dance with the spreading angiosperms.
>
> The southern continents appear to have hosted competitors to therians, too. Paleontologists still know very little about those southern mammals from the late Cretaceous, but provocative new finds suggest that a weird group was prospering: the gondwanatherians

(which, despite their name, were not true therians). For many decades the only records of these mysterious mammals were isolated teeth: high crowned molars with enamel that grows throughout life like those of horses and cows—ideal for grinding tough plant material. In 2014 a team led by David Krause of Stony Brook University unveiled the first skull of a gondwanatherian, which belonged to a new species called *Vintana* that lived in Madagascar in the very latest Cretaceous. It resembled a beaver and possibly fed on some of the first evolving Cretaceous grasses. (*Scientific American,* June 2016, p. 35)

Our ancestors were mammals, and we are mammals. To understand crime, you have to understand that we are mammals—animals.

III

The First Three Minutes

The nitrogen in our DNA, the calcium in our teeth, the iron in our blood...were made in the interiors of collapsing stars. We are made of starstuff....We are a way for the cosmos to know itself.

— Carl Sagan

I NO LONGER BELIEVE in the origin of humans as described in Genesis in the Bible. "The Serpent beguiled me and I did eat" just didn't happen. I like the comments of Dr. Steven Weinberg that begin on page 1 of his book *The First Three Minutes: A Modern View of the Origin of the Universe* as to a Norse myth, particularly since I have Viking roots in my ancestry:

> The origin of the universe is explained in the *Younger Edda*, a collection of Norse myths compiled around 1220 by the Icelandic magnate Snorri Sturleson. In the beginning, says the *Edda*, there was nothing at all. "Earth was not found, nor Heaven above, a Yawning-gap there was, but grass nowhere." To the north and south of nothing lay regions of frost and fire, Niflheim and Musphelheim. The heat from Musphelheim melted some of the frost from Niflheim, and from the liquid drops there grew a giant, Ymer. What did Ymer eat? It seems there was also a cow, Audhumla. And what did *she* eat? Well, there was also some salt. And so on.
>
> I must not offend religious sensibilities, even Viking religious sensibilities, but I think it is fair to say that this is not a very satisfying picture of the origin of the universe. Even leaving aside all

14

objections to hearsay evidence, the story raises as many problems as it answers, and each answer requires a new complication in the initial conditions.

We are not able merely to smile at the *Edda,* and forswear all cosmogonical speculation—the urge to trace the history of the universe back to its beginnings is irresistible. From the start of modern science in the sixteenth and seventeenth centuries, physicists and astronomers have returned again and again to the problem of the origin of the universe.

(See also John Tierney's article in *Newsweek*, January 11, 1988, "The Search for Adam and Eve," pp. 46-52.)

Now, let's back up and begin again with the "Big Bang." Weinberg's *The First Three Minutes* was a 1970s "modern" view of the origin of the universe. It was about a theory of the universe that has grown out of the discovery in 1965 of cosmic microwave radiation.

Weinberg writes that in the beginning there was an explosion ("Big Bang") which occurred simultaneously everywhere, filling all space from the beginning. Every particle of matter rushed apart from every other particle. At about one-hundredth of a second, the temperature of the universe was about a hundred thousand million (1×10^{11}) degrees centigrade. This was so hot that none of the components of ordinary matter—molecules, or atoms, or even the nuclei of atoms—could have been held together.

This explosion consisted of elementary particles which are the subject of high-energy nuclear physics. There were electrons, positrons, neutrons, and light. The universe was filled with light, which consists of particles of zero mass and zero electrical charge known as photons. These particles were continually being created out of energy and then after a short life were annihilated.

The density of this cosmic soup was about four thousand million times that of water at the temperature of a hundred thousand million (1×10^{11}) degrees. There were also heavier particles—protons and neutrons which later formed atomic nuclei. There were about one proton and one neutron for every thousand million nuclear particles (electrons or positrons or neutrinos or photons). The discovery in 1965 of the cosmic radiation background was a measurement of this number.

After about one-tenth of a second, the temperature dropped to thirty thousand million (3×10^{10}) degrees centigrade. After about one second, the temperature was ten thousand million (1×10^{10}) degrees. After about fourteen seconds, the temperature was three thousand million (3×10^9) degrees. Electrons and positrons began to annihilate faster than they could be recreated out of photons and neutrinos. Energy was released.

At the end of the first three minutes, the temperature dropped to one thousand million (1×10^9) degrees. The protons and neutrons began to form complex nuclei, starting with the nucleus of heavy hydrogen (deuterium), which consisted of one proton and one neutron. Light nuclei were able to assemble into helium—two protons and two neutrons. The universe existed mostly in the form of light, neutrinos, and antineutrinos. There was also a small amount of nuclear material of 73 percent hydrogen and 27 percent helium and an equal number of electrons.

The matter continued to rush apart. After a few hundred thousand years, the universe would become cool enough for electrons to join with nuclei to form atoms of hydrogen and helium. The resulting gas would begin to form clumps that would ultimately condense to create galaxies and stars. The stars would begin their life with the ingredients prepared in the first three minutes.

This theory is based on empirical data. The universe

expanded, cooled, and cooked. It may go on expanding forever—getting colder, emptier, and deader. It may contract, breaking up the galaxies and stars and atoms and atomic nuclei into their constituents. What might the *last* three minutes be like?[5]

The first step in the evolution of the elements from hydrogen to helium[6] takes place in young stars (such as our sun) and needs the great heat of the interior. Storms rage on the surface of the sun. What happens in effect is that from time to time a pair of nuclei of heavy hydrogen collides and fuses to make a nucleus of helium. In time, the sun will become mostly helium. And then it will become an even hotter star within which helium nuclei collide to make heavier atoms in turn.

Carbon, for instance, is formed in a star whenever three helium nuclei collide at one spot within less than a millionth of a millionth of a second. Every carbon atom in every living creature has been formed by such a wildly improbable collision. Beyond carbon, oxygen is formed, as well as silicon, sulfur, and heavier elements. The most stable elements are between iron and silver.

It would have been impossible for the stars to build a heavy element like iron, or a super-heavy element like uranium, by the instant assembly of the parts. A star builds hydrogen to helium; then at another stage in a different star, helium is assembled to carbon, to oxygen, to heavy elements;

---

5 See table [Appendix, p. 86]. The sun will burn out and everything on earth will be destroyed. Where will humans—or the next human species— be? Hopefully, we will have moved to another solar system or be on our way.

6 Helium was first identified by a spectrum line during the eclipse of the sun in 1868. It is named after the Greek God of the Sun, Helios, and was not yet known to exist on the earth at that time.

and step by step up the ladder to make ninety-two elements.

This expansion (explosion), known as the "Big Bang," began 14 billion years ago. Our universe is still expanding. The actions of billions of stars in billions of galaxies created all of the elements up to iron on the periodic table, and those of supernovas created more, from iron up to about a total of 100 elements.

Earth, and all the planets in the Milky Way galaxy, were created by these elements that also were used to create all life on earth. The genetic code of DNA for all life on earth including the human animal (mammal) is constructed from these elements: stardust!

> *The division between life and nonlife is perhaps an artificial one.*
>
> — Cyril Ponnamperuma, American Chemist

IV

The Origin of the Universe
and Evolution of Animals

Judge a man by his questions, not his answers.

— Voltaire

*In the beginning, nearly fourteen billion years ago,
all the space and all the matter and all the energy of
the known universe was contained in a volume less
than one-trillionth the size of the period that ends
this sentence.*

— Neil deGrasse Tyson

I MAY BE REPEATING MYSELF, but I do not want to stop and take out the repetition. It's important.

Earth and the other planets in our solar system were formed about 4.5 billion years ago from a cloud of dust and gas swirling around the embryonic sun. A Mars-sized object slammed into the Earth and blasted into space the material that eventually became our moon, leaving a hole in Earth for our oceans and waters to fill.

In 2012, scientists discovered in Greenland (the world's largest island) the oldest fossils ever found—remnants of microbial creatures that lived 3.7 billion years ago. Thus, life appeared very soon after the Earth formed. The age of the rocks was determined through radiometric dating measuring the abundance of elements created by the steady decay of uranium. Such old rocks (older than 3 billion years) are rare.

No one knows how life on Earth began. There is a planet orbiting Proxima Centauri—a red dwarf star that is the sun's closest stellar neighbor—that might also harbor life. Mars is also a place that might harbor extraterrestrial life. In fact, in 1938, with a script based on the H.G. Wells novel *The War of the Worlds*, Orson Welles planned to give America a scare with the Halloween broadcast of The Mercury Theater on the Air. When listeners tuned in, they expected a typical Sunday night radio drama. Three minutes into the program, they heard: "Ladies and gentlemen, we interrupt our program of dance music to bring you a special bulletin." If they had missed Welles' introduction, what followed sounded all too real.

Panic developed in some areas of the country as people were glued to their radios, listening to the unfolding drama of an apparent invasion from Mars. Eventually, New York policemen appeared at the radio studio and tried to get in to stop the broadcast. There was a report of mobs in the streets of at least one Midwestern town. How could the public have been so easily fooled?

It was 1938, and astronomers were still debating the possibility of life on Mars. War in Europe seemed a frightening and real possibility, and the country was still in economic turmoil. Welles took a bit of science and the fears of people who had been through so much and created a believable falsehood.

In October 1994, astronomers discovered the first "brown dwarf" (an object bigger than a planet, smaller than a star) in orbit around the star Gliese 229. Then on July 23, 1995, Thomas Bopp co-discovered a fuzzy object that would become the Great Comet of 1997. He was observing from Stanfield, Arizona, looking at star clusters and galaxies in Sagittarius. Not far away in New Mexico, Alan Hale was observing the same area of sky from his driveway. Hale was a comet hunter, but neither he nor Bopp could imagine how spectacular their find would become.

At the time of their discovery, Comet Hale-Bopp

(C/1995 O1) was some 575 million miles from Earth, well beyond the orbit of Jupiter. Hale and Bopp each pegged the comet at between magnitude 10.5 and 11.0. As Hale-Bopp approached the inner solar system, it brightened steadily. By May 1996, observers could see the comet with the naked eye. And when it passed closest to the sun in April 1997, it was visible even in daylight. The Great Comet would remain visible without optical aid for a record 18 months.

An iron meteorite that's older than the Earth recently streaked through the atmosphere, and scientists tracked it to a remote Australian outback (Gannon, 2016). The 3.7-pound rock, which likely originated in the asteroid belt between Mars and Jupiter, formed during the birth of the solar system more than 4.5 billion years ago. The meteorite was found with the help of a new, high-tech system of 32 automated cameras scattered throughout the vast Australian desert to help scientists spot and track meteors. It was located in the mud near Lake Eyre, just before heavy rains in the area washed away any trace of the impact crater. Geochemical testing on the ancient rock could reveal clues about the Earth's origins and the early history of the solar system.

The "Big Bang" is obviously the beginning of the discussion. The farthest a human can observe is the distance that light has been able to travel during the 14 billion years since the Big Bang expansion began. The most distant visible objects are now about 4×10^{26} meters, or 42 billion light years[7] away. This distance defines our universe. According to Marcelo Gleiser, in his National Public radio (NPR) presentation, "Lessons From Beyond the Heliopause,"

---

7 A light year is used to measure distances within the universe. It is the distance traveled by a photon of light in a vacuum in one year. Light travels at a speed of 300,000 kilometers per second, so a light year is approximately 9.5 trillion miles long. Andromeda, the nearest galaxy to the Milky Way, is at a distance of 2,000 light years.

The sun pours huge quantities of electrically charged particles into space, most of them electrons and protons. This solar wind, as it is called, is confined to a huge bubble known as the heliosphere.

The outer edge of the bubble, the heliopause, marks the transition region beyond which the sun's influence in the interstellar medium becomes negligible. Voyager 1 just crossed this boundary, roughly 100 times more distant from the sun than we are. Even light takes some 14 hours to travel from there to here. (2013)

We know only 5 percent of the composition of the universe. This 5 percent is made of the familiar atoms of the periodic table, their molecular aggregates, or of the components of atoms, protons, electrons, and neutrons. There are also neutrinos—the elusive particles that can traverse matter as if nothing were there, including the whole of Earth. The mystery is the other 95 percent, composed of dark matter (roughly 25 percent) and dark energy (roughly 70 percent). Dark matter doesn't shine and is found around galaxies and clusters of galaxies, like an invisible cloak. We know it's there because it has mass and hence gravity. It pulls on the familiar 5 percent, and we can measure this effect.

Dark energy is much more mysterious—a kind of ether-like medium filling up space with the bizarre property of pushing it apart, making galaxies accelerate from one another. We don't know what either dark matter or dark energy are, but there are hypothetical explanations that try to modify Einstein's theory of gravity to accommodate the observations and do away with the darkness.

There are likely other universes or spheres the same size centered on their planets. They are parallel universes, and each is a part of a larger "multi-universe." This is not metaphysics but physics. This concept of a multi-universe is grounded on well-tested theories such as relativity and quantum mechanics, and it meets the basic criteria of "unphysical" science. There are four distinct types of parallel universes. If you're interested in this, read Max Tegmark's article in *Scientific American*, May 2003, "Parallel Universes."

There is no question the multi-universe exists. Space now appears to be infinite. Everything that is possible becomes real, no matter how improbable. Beyond the range of our telescopes are other regions of space that are identical to ours. This is, today, solid physics. The farthest we can observe is about 42 billion light years, because cosmic expansion has lengthened the distance.

These parallel universes are basically the same as ours. Differences stem from variations in the initial arrangement of matter (Tegmark, 2003). Our universe has space for about 10^{118} subatomic particles. The universe is expanding 96.2 miles per second per megaparsec. Do you understand? (I don't.)

In the book *Smithsonian Intimate Guide to Human Origins,* author Carl Zimmer writes:

> The first half a billion years of Earth's history—from its formation 4,568 billion years ago to four billion years ago—was a time when water rained down to create the oceans, when the first dry land heaved above the surface of the sea to form continents. It was a time when comets and asteroids crashed into Earth, and when a failed planet the size of Mars may have collided with ours, creating the moon from the wreckage. But geologists have very few clues about the timing of these events, such as a few specks of minerals that suggest oceans might have formed before the moon. They find themselves in much the same situation as biographers of ancient Greek philosophers, trying to squeeze as much meaning as they can from scraps of parchment and secondhand stories. (2014)

In that same year, on NPR's *Morning Edition*, Geoff Brumfiel broadcast a piece on Einstein.

Today we know that the universe started with a Big Bang and is still growing. But when Einstein was working on this idea, most people still believed the universe was static and unchanging.... Einstein thought [he] was right. The numbers made sense, because he had made a mathematical mistake. In the middle of a complicated calculation, he wrote a minus sign where he should have written a plus:

Albert Einstein Archives/Hebrew University of Jerusalem, Israel

Einstein screwed up his equations all the time, it turns out. "About 20 percent of Einstein's papers contain various mistakes of various degrees," says Mario Livio, an astrophysicist at the Space Telescope Science Institute.... Livio wrote a book, *Brilliant Blunders*, all about some big mistakes made by great scientists. "You try to think in unconventional ways, and when you do that, guess what: Sometimes you encounter mistakes," Livio says.

Darwin got evolution right, but his ideas on how individual traits were inherited turned out to be way off. And then there's the chemist Linus Pauling, winner of a Nobel Prize: "His model for DNA had almost everything that you can think of wrong with it," says

Livio. "It had three strands instead of two, it was built inside out, and it basically violated some basic rules of chemistry." (2014)

It took two young scientists in the 1950s, Watson and Crick, to describe the double helix of DNA, where great scientists such as Linus Pauling had failed.

A supermassive black hole[8] sits quietly at the center of our galaxy. In an article in *Discover Magazine* called "Rumblings from the Massive Black Hole at the Center of Our Galaxy," Corey S. Powell, science writer, Senior Editor at *Discover*, and adjunct professor of science journalism at NYU's Science and Environmental Reporting Program, writes:

> The beast at the heart of our galaxy lurks so stealthily that for a long time many scientists were not certain it existed at all.
>
> The first hint of that monster came in February 1974, when astronomers Bruce Balick and Robert Brown discovered an unusually compact source of radio waves at the exact center of the Milky Way, some 26,000 light-years away. Brown subsequently named this enigmatic object Sagittarius A* (pronounced "A star"), after the constellation where it appears in the sky. Then came more hints of something strange in the neighborhood: a trickle of X-rays from the same spot; tendrils of agitated gas surrounding it and, most

---

8 I have read that a black hole never goes away, but black holes eventually evaporate and disappear. A black hole is a collapsed star that creates a giant void in space. It only grows larger with time, sucking in anything in its path. What happens to things that enter a black hole is not certain. Stephen Hawking made a career out of the study of these spatial anomalies.

telling, a small group of stars racing around madly for no obvious reason.

Tracking the motions of those stars enabled astronomers to estimate the mass of the unseen object directing the action. From there they built a convincing case that Sagittarius A* was in fact a black hole—the biggest one in the galaxy, with a mass 4.3 million times that of the sun and a diameter of about 25 million kilometers. At the black hole's outer boundary, known as the event horizon, the fabric of space pours inward like a waterfall at the speed of light. Anything caught up in that flow takes a one-way journey to oblivion, winking out of our reality as it crosses the event horizon and then entering an inner realm cut off from the rest of the universe. (2014)

I have no doubt that in reality the future will be vastly more surprising than anything I can imagine. Now my own suspicion is that the Universe is not only queerer than we suppose, but queerer than we can suppose.

— J.B.S. Haldene

In another *Discover Magazine* article, Tim Folger, series editor of The Best American Science and Nature Writing yearly anthology since 2002, writes:

On the remote Kola Peninsula in northwestern Russia, amid the rusting ruins of an abandoned scientific research station, is the deepest hole in the world. Now covered and sealed with a welded metal plate, the Kola Superdeep Borehole, as it's called, is a remnant of a largely forgotten Cold War race that aimed not at the stars, but at Earth's interior.

A team of Soviet scientists began drilling at Kola

in the spring of 1970, with the goal of penetrating as far into Earth's crust as technology would allow. Four years before the Russians started punching their way into the Kola crust, the United States had given up on its own deep-drilling program: Project Mohoe, an attempt to bore miles through the Pacific seafloor and retrieve a sample of the underlying mantle. Mohole fell far short of its target, reaching a depth of just 601 feet after five years of drilling under 11,000 feet of water.

The Soviets were more persistent. Their work at Kola continued for 24 years—the project outlived the Soviet Union itself. Before drilling ended in 1994, the team hit a layer of 2.7-billion-year-old rock, almost a billion years older than the Vishnu schist at the base of the Grand Canyon. Temperatures at the bottom of the Kola hole exceeded 300 degrees Fahrenheit; the rocks were so plastic that the hole started to close whenever the drill was withdrawn....

And the depth of the Kola hole after 24 years of drilling? About 7.6 miles—deeper than an inverted Mount Everest and roughly halfway to the mantle, but still a minuscule distance, considering Earth's 7,918-mile diameter. If Earth were the size of an apple, the Kola hole wouldn't even break through the skin.

All the mines on Earth, all the tunnels, caves, and chasms, all the seas, and all of life exist within or on top of the thin shell of our planet's rocky crust, which is much thinner, comparatively, than an eggshell. Earth's immense, deep interior—the mantle and core—has never been directly explored.... Everything we know about the mantle, which begins about 15 miles below the surface, and about Earth's core, 1,800 miles beneath us, has been gleaned remotely.

While our understanding of the rest of the universe grows almost daily, knowledge of the inner workings of our own world advances far more slowly. "Going into space is just a lot easier than going down for an equivalent distance," says David Stevenson, a geophysicist at the California Institute of Technology. "Going down from 5 kilometers to 10 is much harder than going from zero to 5."[9]

What scientists do know is that life on Earth's surface is profoundly affected by what happens at inaccessible depths. Heat from Earth's inner core, which is as hot as the surface of the sun, churns an outer core of molten iron and nickel, generating a magnetic field that deflects lethal cosmic and solar radiation away from the planet. For a glimpse of what Earth might be like without its protective magnetic shield, we have only to look at the lifeless surfaces of worlds with anemic magnetic fields, like Mars and Venus.

The planetary architecture that provides Earth's sheltering field has been broadly understood for several decades now: a solid-iron inner core roughly the size of the moon, surrounded by a 1,400-mile-thick outer core of liquid iron and nickel, with 1,800 miles of solid mantle above, topped by a crust of slowly drifting tectonic plates. But when it comes to the very center of the planet, this blueprint is sorely incomplete.

"Right at this moment, there is a problem with our understanding of Earth's core," says Stevenson, "and it's something that's emerged only over the last year or two. The problem is a serious one. We do not now understand how the Earth's magnetic field has lasted for billions of years. We know that the Earth has had a magnetic field for most of its history. We don't know how the Earth did that.... We have less of

---

9 By the way, a space vehicle must move at a rate of at least 7 miles per second to escape Earth's gravitational pull.

an understanding now than we thought a decade ago of how the Earth's core has operated throughout history." (Folger, 2014)

To add to the mystery, the North Pole is losing about 30,000 square miles of sea ice per year. But at the South Pole, the sea ice has been growing, hitting a 35-year record of 19 million square miles. Why are the Arctic and Antarctic such polar opposites? The question is all the more puzzling since ice shelves along Antarctica's coast are melting. Now research suggests the answer can be found blowing in the winds that swirl around the South Pole.

University of Washington oceanographer Jinlun Zhang created a computer simulation revealing that the winds push floating layers of sea ice together, compressing them into thick ridges that are slower to melt. And as the ice layers merge, they expose areas of open water to the frigid air, which leads to the formation of even more ice (Lewis, 2013).

LIFE ON EARTH

Let's go back to life on Earth. As stated, during the Cretaceous period 65 million years ago, mammals were doing well. Then the asteroid hit Earth, unleashing wildfires, tsunamis, earthquakes, and volcanic eruptions. This was too much for the dinosaurs that had been around for 180 million years.

Mammals also felt the pang of extinction. Many larger mammals became extinct with the dinosaurs. But some survived (obviously). In 1908, a Neanderthal skeleton was found in a cave near the village of La Chapelle-aux-Saints in south-central France. (In 1863, Neanderthals had been given their own species designation: *Homo neanderthalensis*.) This skeleton is evidence of evolution and human origin. Read *Seven Skeletons: The Evolution of the World's Most*

Famous Human Fossils (2016) by Lydia Pyne (University of Texas at Austin).

Neanderthals built structures; had sophisticated hunting strategies, fire-starting technologies, and art; and they buried their dead. According to DNA studies, Neanderthals interbred with us (*Homo sapiens*), and the more we study our Pleistocene relative, the more their behavior seems similar to ours. But did they have a definition of crime?

What happened to the Neanderthals? Our own ancestors—recognizably modern people and traditionally known as Cro-Magnons—were in Europe around 40,000 years ago. We also know that the Neanderthals hung on in Europe until at least 35,000 years ago. So the two species of human lived side by side for at least 5,000 years and perhaps for more than 10,000 years.

In his book, *Neanderthals, Bandits and Farmers: How Agriculture Really Began*, Colin Tudge writes:

> It seems that human beings of the genus *Homo* first appeared around two million years ago. And the first anatomically human beings—people who would have looked perfectly at home in a bus queue—appeared on this Earth something over 100,000 years ago in Africa.... The first people that really seem to impress the palaeo-anthropologists are those of the late Palaeolithic, of around 40,000 years ago....They began producing a greater range of tools and refining the designs, and they began serious cave-painting.... The first bona fide farmers—or at least proto-farmers—appeared at this time too.
>
> The point is not to put a precise date on this transition, but to note that human beings virtually throughout their two million year history have not merely been 'hunters and gatherers', the way that these terms are generally understood but have always

manipulated their environment in various ways that increased their food supply....

All the main grades of hominid arose in Africa. *Ardipithecus* appeared in Africa about five million years ago—*Australophithesus*, a little later. The first *Homo* in the form of *Homo habilis* appeared more than two million years ago. *Homo erectus* appeared about two million years ago and was the first hominid to migrate out of Africa, perhaps around 1.5 million years ago. Around the same time *Homo ergaster* appeared, who was perhaps the ancestor of later humans. *Homo heidelbergensis*, formerly known as 'archaic *Homo sapiens*,' who also migrated out of Africa, perhaps about half a million years ago, was the ancestor both of *Homo neanderthalensis* and of *Homo sapiens*; and *Homo sapiens* first appeared in anatomically modern form around 100,000 years ago. But around 40,000 years ago, in late Palaeolithic times, the migrations became even more impressive, as people learned to build boats and crossed the open sea. Thus around 40,000 years ago people entered Australia for the first time, from South East Asia, and by at least 30,000 years ago had begun to populate the Pacific islands. Around 13,000 years ago, people first entered the Americas— not in fact by sailing, but by walking across the land bridge commonly referred to as Beringia, which formed between Siberia and Alaska during the Ice Ages, when the sea level fell by up to 200 meters....

The first unequivocal intimation of farming that the archaeological record provides is from the Middle East of around 10,000 years ago. So what was happening then to have caused such a jolt in the culture?

Answer: The latest Ice Age was coming to an end. We are used to the notion that Ice Ages are studied by geologists, while the lives of modern human beings—

and these were modern people—are the province of archaeologists and historians....

The crucial factor is what happened to the sea. During Ice Ages any water that falls on land stays there. Huge tracts of North America were under ice that in places was several miles deep. So much water is locked on land that the sea level fall by up to 200 meters. During the most recent Ice Age, Beringia—the land bridge between Alaska and Siberia—was as large as Poland. That is how people crossed from one continent to the other—together with the elk, moose and bison that are now the principal large ungulates in North America. During the most recent Ice Age, too, the great shallow sea that now lies between Saudi Arabia and Iran was not there; the present-day Persian Gulf was dry land.

And the land in what is now the Persian Gulf must have been a very favored spot, where the Tigris and the Euphrates, which now define Mesopotamia alias Iraq, would have flowed together, and out into the Arabian Sea. The land was flat and the climate balmy. There was no shortage of water. There would have been fish and shellfish galore, and great flocks of water birds, with gazelles and fallow deer and fruiting trees. This would have been the place where the people congregated....

Ever since that time the human population has been rising exponentially, from an estimated eight million worldwide around 10,000 years ago, to between one hundred and three hundred million at the time of Christ, to six billion—6,000 million—by 2000 AD. (1999)

As of January 2019, the website Worldometers reports that there are 7.7 billion people on the planet ("World population").

In the century after the first humans arrived from Asia

in North America, many large mammals have disappeared, including horses, camels, giant beavers, American pigs, elephants (including mammoths and mastodons), giant ground sloths, and the glyptodont (armadillo the size of a bread van), plus the animals that preyed upon them (saber-tooth cats, wolves, and giant bears).

V

Stop and Critically Think

The mind is like a parachute. It only operates when it is open.

— Unknown

MY ANALYSIS has not been complete or perfect. What is important is to understand the evolutionary journey of the mammal is (so far) 200 million years long. Remember: Sixty-five million years ago, a huge asteroid hit the Earth, unleashing wildfires, tsunamis, earthquakes, and volcanic eruptions. Dinosaurs that had prevailed for 180 million years were gone.

Mammals also felt the pain of extinction, but some survived. Molecular clock studies which calculate when distant ancestors diverged from one another based on DNA differences in living species show that common ancestors of placentals (that's us) evolved alongside the dinosaurs in the Cretaceous period. These mammals split into major subgroups, including rodents and primates.

The death of the dinosaurs was instrumental in the rise of the mammal. It was the spark that ignited a placental revolution. Placentals took over the planet. Evolution in the next 60 million years would turn small proto-primitives into bipedal-walking philosophizing apes—us!

So where did crime come from? A crime by definition is any social harm defined and made punishable by law. But what causes crime? Sigmund Freud (1856-1939)[10] said that the principal task of civilization is to protect man from

---

10 Sigmund Freud died in 1939 at the age of 83. His scientific contributions have been ranked by some with Plank and Einstein.

nature. So, what is nature? I'll continue my discussion.

Through the study of DNA differences in living species and fossils, scientists have established some of our ancestors—for example, *Torrejonia*, a puppy-sized creature with gangly limbs and long fingers and toes who leaped through trees—a distant cousin of ours (a placental) who lived 63 million years ago. What did they know about crime?

According to Jerry Coyne, an evolutionary biologist at the University of Chicago and author of *Why Evolution Is True*, the evidence is "overwhelming" that Darwin's idea of natural selection is true. There are now six biological hot spots or locations in the world where evolution is clear, but none of them answer my question about the cause of crime. Or do they?

About 540 million years ago simple, single-celled life developed into a variety of multicellular forms (McGowan, 2014). There was a sudden and explosive diversification of animal life from an unknown trigger. There was no concept of crime in the beginning. Or was there?

The theory of evolution is no longer questioned by 99 percent or more of scientists and experts. I call biological evolution "Darwinian evolution," but Alfred Richard Wallace (1823-1913) must also be recognized.

In his twenties, Charles Darwin had been offered a job as naturalist on a survey ship, the *Beagle*, which set sail December 22, 1831. His job would be to map the coast of South America. He spent five years on this ship, and on this voyage he met the natives of South America at Tierra del Fuego.

In 1838, as he was returning to England, he had a thought: Animals must compete to survive; nature acts as a selective force, killing the weak and creating new species from the survivors who were fitted to their environment. He had found an explanation for the evolution of species by natural selection, and he now had a theory to work. For years, Darwin did not reduce his theory to paper, but in 1842, he drafted in pencil 35 pages. In 1844, he expanded his draft to 230 pages in ink. He deposited that draft to his wife (with money) with instructions to publish it if he died.

Three centuries earlier, Archbishop James Ussher of Armagh (1551-1656) had said that the universe was created in 4004 B.C. Armed as he was with dogma and ignorance, he brooked no rebuttal. He or another cleric "knew" the year, the date, the day of the week, the hour. But the puzzle of the age of the world had remained a paradox well into the 1900s. While it was by then clear to scientists that the earth was millions of years old, Darwin knew that he was saying something deeply shocking to the public. He would have liked to have died before his theory was published. He refused to argue in public. He did not want to meet the public.

Wallace, one year younger than Darwin, had been a land-surveyor. He became interested in plants and insects, and this shaped his life. (He did not have a university education and had to work for a living.) In 1848, at the age of 25, Wallace decided to become a naturalist. He would collect specimens to sell to museums and English collectors. He sailed with a friend to South America and then a thousand miles up the Amazon and then up the Rio Negro. The local Indians helped him.

Wallace spent four years in the Amazon basin, and then he spent eight years in the Malay archipelago collecting specimens of wildlife. Of course, as a naturalist, Wallace wondered how all this variety of life had come about.

In 1855, Wallace published an essay entitled *On the Law Which Has Regulated the Introduction of New Species*, in which he discussed observations regarding the geographic and geologic distribution of both living and fossil species. He continued to ponder his observations, and one night on the small volcanic island of Ternate in the

Moluccas, Spice Islands, between New Guinea and Borneo, he had a flash of insight. He returned from the tropics as Darwin had done, convinced that related species diverged from a common stock.

On June 18, 1858, Charles Darwin received a paper sent to him by Wallace, who was hoping it could be published. Darwin was at a loss to know what to do. For twenty careful, silent years he had marshaled facts to support his theory on the evolution of species, and now there fell on his desk from nowhere a paper by Wallace on the same subject.

Lyle and Hooker, friends of Darwin who by now had seen some of his work, arranged that Wallace's paper and one by Darwin should be read in the absence of both at the next meeting of the Linnean Society in London the following month.[11] The papers made no stir at all. But Darwin's hand had been forced. Wallace was, as Darwin described him, "generous and noble." And so Darwin put aside his fears and wrote *On the Origin of Species*, publishing it at the end of 1859. It was instantly a sensation and best-seller.

There were thus two different explanations independent of each other. The theory of evolution was conceived by two men independent of each other, living at the same time in the same culture—the culture of Queen Victoria of England. Wallace had gone to the unknown forests of the Amazon in South America to the East Indies, and Darwin went by way of South America to the islands of the coast in the Pacific.

---

11 From their website, "The Linnean Society of London is the world's oldest active biological society. Founded in 1788 by Sir James Edward Smith (1759–1828), who was its first President. The Society takes its name from the Swedish naturalist Carl Linnaeus (1707–1778) whose botanical, zoological and library collections have been in its keeping since 1829.... As it moves into its third century the Society provides a continuous forum for the discussion and advancement of the life sciences. It was at a meeting of the Society in 1858 that papers from Charles Darwin and Alfred Russel Wallace outlining the theory of evolution by natural selection were first presented."

Darwin and Wallace both get credit for a theory of evolution by natural selection, but I'll still call it Darwinian evolution.

HUMANS ARE CHIMPANZEES

Keep reading. I understand your reaction, but open your mind for a few minutes.

Humans are animals. Humans are mammals. And humans are chimpanzees. The DNA of the common chimp and of the pigmy chimp is 98.4 percent identical to the third chimpanzee—humans (Spencer, 2015). The common chimp is called *Homo troglodytes*. The pigmy chimp is *Homo paniscus*, and the human chimp is *Homo sapiens*. What difference does it make? It helps us understand evolution, who we are, and our behavior—good and bad. Chimps are dishonest and lie, cheat, and steal. They are killers. So are we, because we are chimps. (All men are sinners.)

According to the Bible, Adam and Eve disobeyed God. Their son Cain killed Abel. We are all descendants of this murderer. The sperm of Adam contained "original sin" that has been passed on to all generations—males and females. "Free will" is not mentioned in the Bible. Infants don't have "free will." The mentally ill do not have "free will." Genetically defective humans do not have "free will." Do you choose your skin color? Do you choose your sex?

I argue no one has "free will" any more than a snake, a dog, or any mammal including, of course, our "cousins" the chimpanzees. The Garden of Eden is a myth. "Free will" is the product of the imagination of well-meaning Jewish and Christian scholars. The words are not in Genesis nor anywhere in the Bible. These scholars probably actually believed their conclusion about free will and the Garden of Eden, but they were dead wrong.

DOES THIS CHILD HAVE FREE WILL?

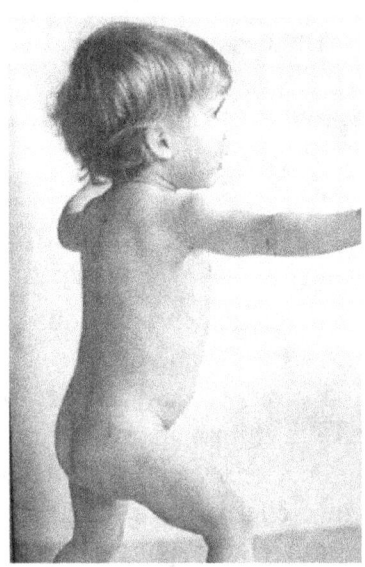

VI

The Cause of Crime

The only thing harder than getting a new idea into the...mind is to get an old one out.

— B.H. Liddell Hart

I SAY THE CAUSE of crime is in DNA, the stuff of all animal life. The first human genome sequence was published in 2001: 3 billion As, Cs, Ts, and Gs. We still don't know the molecular wiring diagram for human cells, cures for disease, or crime. Humans and chimpanzees are close relatives based on DNA, but chimpanzees are not afflicted with the same diseases, and some are less severe. What about crime?

In 2005, the chimpanzee genome was finally published (Spencer, 2005). The genomes of other vertebrate animals have since then been published. Can we now establish the genetic basis (or epigenetic) for all the traits or characteristics that make us human by scanning regions of DNA and comparing the findings?[12] Including crime?

Biology is to crime as physics is to baseball. In a *Scientific American* article (June 2013), Michael Sherman discussed Adrian Raine's book, *The Anatomy of Violence: The Biological Roots of Crime*:

---

12 "Lies, damned lies, and statistics" was a phrase popularized in the United States by Mark Twain. Obviously, decisions affecting millions of humans should be made using the best possible information. Researchers, public officials, and anyone using statistics to draw conclusions from data need to test the results. Statistical investigations can result in errors. Beware, of course, of results that haven't been repeated or that depend on a single method of measurement. Samuel Langhorne Clemens (1835-1910), or "Mark Twain," was a journalist in Nevada before becoming America's foremost humorist.

Do criminals look different from noncriminals? Are there patterns that science can discover to enable society to identify potential felons before they break the law or to rehabilitate them after? University of Pennsylvania criminologist and psychiatrist Adrian Raine attempts to answer these and related questions in his book *The Anatomy of Violence: The Biological Roots of Crime....* Raine details how evolutionary psychology and neuroscience are converging in this effort. For example, he contrasts two cases that show new ways to look at the origins of wrongdoing. First is the example of "Mr. Oft," a perfectly normal man turned into a pedophile by a massive tumor at the base of his orbitofrontal cortex; when it was resected, he returned to normalcy. Second, we learn of a murderer-rapist named Donta Page, whose childhood was so horrifically bad—he was impoverished, malnourished, fatherless, abused, raped and beaten on the head to the point of being hospitalized several times—that his brain scan "showed clear evidence of reduced functioning in the medial and orbital regions of the prefrontal cortex."

The significance of these examples is revealed when Raine reviews the brain scans he made of 41 murderers, in which he found significant impairment of their prefrontal cortex. Such damage "results in a loss of control over the evolutionary more primitive parts of the brain, such as the limbic system, that generate raw emotions like anger and rage." Research on neurological patients in general, Raine adds, shows that "damage done to the prefrontal cortex results in [increased] risk-taking, irresponsibility, and rule-breaking behavior," along with personality changes such as "impulsivity, loss of self-control, and an inability to modify and inhibit behavior appropriately" and cognitive impairment such as a "loss of intellectual flexibility and poorer problem-solving skills" that may later result in "school failure, unemployment, and economic deprivation, all factors that predispose someone to a criminal and violent way of life."

What is the difference between an aggressive tumor and a violent upbringing? One is clearly biological, whereas the other results from a complex web of biosocial factors. Yet, Raine points out, both can lead to troubling moral and legal questions: "If you agree that Mr. Oft was not responsible for his actions because it was orbitofrontal tumor, what judgment would you render on someone who committed the same act as Mr. Oft but, rather than having a clearly visible tumor, had a subtle prefrontal pathology with a neurodevelopmental origin that was hard to see visually from a PET scan?" A tumor is quickly treatable, but an upbringing—not so much.

We also need an evolutionary psychology of violence and aggression. "From rape to robbery and even to theft, evolution has made violence and antisocial behavior a profitable way of life for a small minority of the population," Raine writes. Theft can grant the perpetrator more resources necessary for survival and reproduction. A reputation for being aggressive can grant males higher status in the pecking order of social dominance. Revenge murders are an evolved strategy for dealing with cheaters and free riders....

An evolutionary psychology and neuroscience of criminology is the next and necessary step toward producing a more moral world. In Raine's concluding remarks, he exhorts us to "rise above our feelings of retribution, reach out for rehabilitation, and engage in a more humane discourse on the causes of violence." Although some people may balk at the biological determinism inherent in such an approach and others may recoil from the preference for rehabilitation over retribution, we can all benefit from a scientific understanding of the true causes of crime. (p. 90)

Raine's book is indeed amazing. His research is mind-boggling. However, I have changed my opinion over the years and believe the cause of crime is not just defective brains and/or life experience. I now believe that all humans are simply "criminals" or have the potential for crime because they are animals—mammals. We simply inherit these tendencies, traits, or characteristics, but civilization changed the rules of behavior by defining crime to require punishment for rule violators—a big mistake.

VII

Epigenetics and Genetics

"When I use a word," Humpty Dumpty said, in rather a scornful tone, "it means just what I choose it to mean—nothing more nor less."

"The question is," said Alice, "whether you can make words mean so many different things."

"The question is," said Humpty Dumpty, "which is to be master—that's all."

— Lewis Carroll, *Through the Looking Glass and What Alice Found There*

EPIGENETICS is a new science. Genes can be affected not only by DNA mutations but also by "epigenetics." These effects alter gene "behavior" without changing the genetic code. (Genes mutate with each new generation.) Such changes can last a lifetime. But these effects are reversible. For example, we now know cancer is as much an epigenetic disease as genetic (Fymat, 2017). Also, how does a ball of identical stem cells become a person? (Stem cells have genetic and epigenetic properties.)

What does the word "epigenetics" actually mean? In a special Summer 2011 issue of *Discover Magazine* called "Evolution: Rethinking the Story of Life," editor Kat McGowan writes, "Scientists have only begun to wrap their heads around epigenetics, the way DNA can be chemically modified in response to diet, stress, or other environmental factors in ways that permanently change how genes are activated."

These changes can also be passed on to the next generation. For instance, your children's genes might be affected by the things you ate and the things you smoked.

Rapid progress in DNA-sequencing technology, leading to powerful new techniques, promises to upend our understanding of the machinery of evolution, the way that changes are encoded in genes and expressed in living forms.

Epigenetics is helping to unravel the complicated relationship between our genes and our environment. Researchers have argued for decades whether specific personality characteristics and illness are a result of our genes (nature) or environment (nurture). It has become clear that, in fact, both genes and the environment constantly interact to make us who we are and produce illnesses such as depression.

Studies in epigenetics have revealed that certain environmental influences can actually make changes to our genes that affect how they function and that these changes can go on to be inherited by our offspring. When I started writing the manuscript to *Understanding Crime*, I planned to explain "epigenetics." I can't. It's too complex. Read some books, such as Dr. Richard C. Francis's book on epigenetics (see below) or one of the other books by other authors on this new science. Try to master it yourself. It includes so much, and it turned my thinking upside down!

So, I've changed my mind. The cause of crime (all behavior) is a product of DNA and epigenetics. Epigenetics is complex. Epigenetics is challenging to understand. Epigenetics deserves your attention, and in the world tomorrow we will most likely know more about crime and epigenetics as well as more about human life. What will we learn?

Following is Dr. Francis's description of the themes of his book *Epigenetics: How Environment Shapes Our Genes* (2011):

The first theme concerns the nature of epigenetic processes: a form of gene regulation. Epigenetic gene regulation is long-term gene regulation, hence epigenetic alterations have long-term effects on gene behavior. Indeed, epigenetic alterations of gene behavior can be longer lasting than mutational alterations of gene behavior. But unlike the alterations of gene behavior caused by mutations, epigenetic alterations of gene behavior are generally reversible.

The second theme is that our environment affects the behavior of our genes, both in the short and the long term. The long-term environmental influences on genes' behavior come by way of epigenetic processes. Environmentally induced epigenetic alterations that occur early in our lives are especially important. We have explored, in particular, the epigenetic effects of poor nutrition and stress on the fetus and the infant, and their myriad health consequences during adulthood. But our environment continues to epigenetically influence our genes throughout our lives.

The third theme is randomness. Epigenetic processes, like all biological processes, have a random element, and sometimes this random element looms large. This is true, for example, of methylation at the agouti locus, which affects not only coloration but susceptibility to obesity, diabetes, and cancer in mice. X-chromosome inactivation is another epigenetic process for which randomness is critical. Indeed, in this case, we could say that the randomness is adaptive. Without it there certainly wouldn't be any X-women.

Clones, whether natural as in monozygotic twins, or manufactured as in Cc the calico cat, are far from carbon copies. There are a number of reasons for this, some of them epigenetic. In the case of Cc, random X-chromosome inactivation caused her coloration to diverge markedly from that of her mother, to the point that she even lacked one pigment entirely.... Other examples of clone discordance include Alzheimer's disease, lupus, cancer, and color discrimination.

Some epigenetic alterations of gene behavior have effects that extend beyond an individual lifetime. This is theme number four. The effect of these transgenerational epigenetic alterations may be direct or indirect. Direct transgenerational effects occur when the epigenetic mark is transmitted directly from parent to offspring, through sperm or egg. This is what I call "true epigenetic inheritance." True epigenetic inheritance is not common in mammals like us, but it does occur. Indirect transgenerational effects are much more common.

The most direct of these indirect transgenerational epigenetic effects is genomic imprinting, in which the original epigenetic mark in the parent is reproduced with great fidelity in the offspring. Much more indirect are the transgenerational effects observed in the maternal behavior and stress response of rats. Here, the epigenetic alterations that influence these behaviors are recreated through the social interactions that they both influence and are influenced by. This transgenerational effect is a positive feedback loop involving gene action and social interaction. Whether direct or indirect, these transgenerational epigenetic effects should expand our notion of inheritance.

The fifth and final theme is actually a meta-theme, a theme comprised of the previous four themes. This meta-theme concerns some of our basic intuitions about the role of genes in explaining biological processes ranging from protein synthesis to cellular differentiation and cancer. Genes are traditionally viewed as biochemical executives that initiate and direct these processes, in contradistinction to all other biochemicals within a cell, which function in a more blue-collar way. I used the metaphor of the theatrical production, the play, to illustrate this view: Genes are the directors, proteins the actors, and all other biochemicals act as stagehands. From an alternative perspective, advocated here, this play is more improvisational and genes are more like members of an ensemble cast, a cast that includes proteins and other biochemical actors. Gene actions are as much effect as cause during protein synthesis, and genomic activity is as much effect as cause during cellular differentiation, both normal and pathological.

From this alternative perspective, genes have two faces, two aspects like the Roman deity Janus, the god of doorways and gates, of entryways and exits, of beginnings and endings. Only one aspect, the outward-facing, casual aspect, is acknowledged on the traditional account. The result is a simplistic and distorted view of genes and gene actions. For genes also have another aspect, the inward-facing, responsive aspect. This responsive aspect of the Janus gene is highlighted in epigenetic research, the payoffs of which, even in these early days, have been enormous.

Like Raine's book *The Anatomy of Violence: The Biological Roots of Crime*, I found Dr. Francis's book *Epigenetics: How Our Environment Shapes Our Genes* mind-boggling! Read it.

There have been recent innovations in DNA sequencing technology and new computational methods that allow scientists to see more and more. All life on earth is composed of atoms. Atoms are composed of neutrons and protons (in the nucleus), with electrons that seem to swirl around outside the nucleus in specific orbits. It has been discovered that atoms have many parts or particles—266 or more. (Most of our universe is "dark matter" and is invisible! The particles of dark matter cannot yet be identified.)

In 2012, the Higgs boson (a particle in the atom) was discovered at CERN's Large Hadron Collider (LHC) near Geneva. Higgs had been predicted in the 1960s. It was said to be the final missing piece of the puzzle. In physics, the "Standard Model" describes the known particles and forces in physics. Finding the Higgs particle vindicated the Standard Model.

To understand the nature of the universe, study atoms. There are four fundamental forces in the universe. To understand one of these four (known as the "weak four") you study the "neutron." How long does it live? The neutron is prone to radioactive decay.[13] Inside the atomic nucleus, it can survive for a long time and may never decay. On its own, it will transform into other particles within 15 minutes, more or less.

Scientists have not been able to accurately measure neutron life. It is a puzzle, but it is vital for an understanding of the nature of the universe. The survival time of the neutron

---

13 "Despite decades of trying, scientists have not been able to definitively measure how long neutrons live outside of atomic nuclei— the best experiments in the world produce conflicting results. Although the length of the neutron lifetime is undetermined, the cause of neutron decay is well known. Through a process called beta decay, a neutron transforms into a proton and releases an electron and an antineutrino, the antimatter counterpart to the neutrino particle. The decay ensures that the final particles' charge and spin angular momentum tally to equal those of the original particle." (Greene & Geltenbort, 2016, p. 39, including graphic below).

determined how the lightest chemical element first formed after the Big Bang. Cosmologists have used this information to calculate the expected abundance of the elements, etc. (These studies are beyond the scope of this paper.)

The insight would deepen our understanding of the laws of nature and their implication for the origin and evolution of the universe. Perhaps crime? In my opinion, the true cause of crime is a matter of physics and biology.

Man is a predatory animal. Big fish eat little fish: the food chain. Consider the behavior of animals around us. We all have the "same" DNA. Consider the behavior of animals before and since 65 million years ago. Consider the behavior of Caveman.

Imagine living in a cave 40,000 years ago with 15 men and five women. These 20 humans are "governed" by an extremely mean, dangerous, male leader. What he says goes—sex, everything. Dogs have bonded with humans, and together they search for animals and kill to eat. It is a cruel world. There are no recorded definitions of crime. Survive and reproduce. That's it.

VIII

Neurobiological Defenses
and Mitigation of Punishment

*Man's predecessors differed from living apes in being
confirmed killers; carnivorous creatures, that seized
living quarries by violence, battered them to death,
tore apart their broken bodies, dismembered them
limb from limb, slaking their ravenous thirst with
the hot blood of victims and greedily devouring livid
writhing flesh.*

— Raymond Dart

*We are Cain's children.... Man is a predator whose
natural instinct is to kill with a weapon. The sudden
addition of the enlarged brain to the equipment of an
armed already-successful predatory animal created...
the human being.*

— Robert Ardrey

WHEN ARE WE RESPONSIBLE for our actions and when
are we in the grip of biological forces beyond our control? I
answer we are always in the grip of biological forces beyond
our control. Behavioral biology, the interactions of the brain,
mind, body, our environment, supports my answer—I think.
(One example: aggressive impulses.) The brain is sculpted
by evolution, constrained or freed by genes, shaped by life
experiences, modulated by hormones, and influenced to
produce our behavior (Sapolsky, 2005). Remember: Our
ancestors were predatory animals that demonstrated their
prowess by killing.

Suppose a criminal defense lawyer has no defense.

Suppose his client will not "plead guilty" and rejects a plea bargain. What does the lawyer do? None of the traditional defenses apply to the facts of the case. What about a biological defense? Remember, most jurors (90 percent) believe in the Garden of Eden, Adam and Eve, and "free will." They believe that Genesis 2-3 introduces the concept of "free will" in the Garden of Eden and that God created man (Adam and Eve) out of nothing (*ex nihilo*) or out of pre-existent matter as some interpreters believe. They believe that the snake in the Garden of Eden was Satan!

Most Jews and Christians would therefore be poor jurors if the defense was biological or if the issue was biological mitigation of punishment. In 50-200 years, we will know the relationship of the conscious mind and the unconscious, and crime will be explained at the molecular level. Will "jurors" then be able to set aside religious beliefs?

In the meantime, there may be no other choice. If the defense lawyer cannot consider such a defense because of his beliefs, he should withdraw. As a matter of ethics, professional responsibility, and the Sixth Amendment, it does not matter what the defense lawyer personally believes. As a matter of duty, he must consider the best defense regardless of personal beliefs.

The King James Version of the Bible was first published in 1611 for English-speaking people in Britain and the entire world. However, by the late 19th century or in the 20th century, there were many other English translations as opposed to Hebrew, Greek, or Latin (Catholic).

According to Gary A. Rendsburg, Ph.D., Professor of Jewish Studies at Rutgers University:

> The most widely used Bible in college classrooms is the Revised Standard Version, which comes in a variety of editions, such as the New Oxford Annotated Bible. This translation adheres closely to the Hebrew

original, word for word.

The Jewish Publication Society Version (technically the New Jewish Publication Society Version, because an older one was produced in 1916) is the standard among Jewish readers of the Bible. Note that it is a more idiomatic rendering and frequently departs from the Hebrew text literally. A recent edition, which includes this translation, is The Jewish Study Bible.

Robert Alter, a professor at the University of California at Berkeley, produced a translation of the book of Genesis alone in 1996, replete with superb notes of a literary nature; he then completed the task for the entire Torah, published in 2004.

The most literal translation of the Torah, which of course, includes the book of Genesis, is that of Everett Fox, professor at Clark University in Worcester, MA. For those readers who wish to get as close to the Hebrew text as possible, with the result that the English is often a bit odd-sounding, this is the text for you. (2006)

Regardless, Adam and Eve are said to have violated God's word by eating the fruit of the Tree of Knowledge of Good and Evil. Adam and Eve had "free will" and could make their own decision to eat the fruit and violate God's command.

"Free will" is not a phrase in the text. But Jews and Christians both read the text as if it were in the Bible. Theologians teach and believe this casts the responsibility for evil in the world onto mankind for not following God's command. (Read Genesis 2-3.) I do not agree. God may have been the Creator, but the Garden of Eden is a myth. While working on a research paper entitled "Lawyers and the Puritans" (early 1600 England), I discovered the truth about King James I—father of the authorized revised version of the Bible, its translation into English. He was a scoundrel!

Here's what John Tierney wrote in the *Wall Street Journal*, June 9, 2017, in an article called "The Tyranny of the Administrative State":

> James, who reigned in England from 1603 through 1625, claimed that divinely granted "absolute power" authorized him to suspend laws enacted by Parliament or dispense with them for any favored person....
>
> James also made his own laws, bypassing Parliament and the courts by issuing proclamations and using his "royal prerogative" to establish commissions and tribunals. He exploited the infamous Star Chamber, a court that got its name from the gilded stars on its ceiling.
>
> "The Hollywood version of the Star Chamber is a torture chamber where the walls were speckled with blood," Mr. Hamburger [Phillips Hamburger, Constitutional scholar] says. "But torture was a very minor part of its business. It was very bureaucratic. Like modern administrative agencies, it commissioned expert reports, issued decrees and enforced them. It had regulations controlling the press, and it issued rules for urban development, environmental matters and various industries.
>
> James's claims were rebuffed by England's chief justice, Edward Coke, who in 1610 declared that the king "by his proclamation cannot create any offense which was not an offense before." The king eventually dismissed Coke, and expansive royal powers continued to be exercised by James and his successor, Charles I. The angry backlash ultimately prompted Parliament to abolish the Star Chamber and helped provoke a civil war that ended with the beheading of Charles in 1649.
>
> A subsequent king, James II, took the throne in 1685 and tried to reassert the prerogative power. But

he was dethroned in the Glorious Revolution of 1688, which was followed by Parliament's adoption of a bill of rights limiting the monarch and reasserting the primacy of Parliament and the courts. That history inspired the American Constitution's limits on the executive branch....

SCIENCE VERSUS RELIGION

Enough about King James and his Bible. I believe in science.

A molecule in science is the smallest possible piece of a substance that can be identified as that substance. Invisible forces attract one molecule to another to become an identifiable substance. Receptors are molecules made of proteins made of amino acids. A typical neuron in the brain may have millions of receptors on its surface. Ligands (from the Latin *ligare*, "that which binds," the same root as religion) are molecules that specifically bind to the receptors of other (usually larger) molecules, such as neurotransmitters and steroids, and in so doing convey an informational message to the cell (Pert, 350). Peptides make up 95 percent of all ligands.

Modern humans entered Europe 40,000 years ago. They had the same brain(s) that we have: cells, molecules, DNA, genes, proteins, etc. Human brains were divided into two sides: left and right, then as now. They were and are connected. But no one today can actually explain the human decision-making process of today or then!

Vikings were fearsome marauders who struck terror in the hearts of their victims beginning in 1793. Vikings from Norway, Denmark, and Sweden raided England, Ireland, and Scotland. They had the same brain(s) that we have. Cavemen, our ancestors before the Vikings, had the same brain(s). The chemistry of nucleic acids (DNA & RNA) and their operational agents, proteins, is the same today as it was when men lived in caves and had no written, defined crimes.

Homo erectus and *Homo habilis*, both now extinct, were different species from *Homo sapiens* but of the same genus (*Homo*). How did they make decisions? Well, the same as we do, but with less knowledge and with no written law or rules for criminal behavior.

The principal of biology that distinguishes the biological from physical science is Darwin's evolution by natural selection. (Biology is more like history than physics.) We survived. We are the only hominid species that survived. But I'll bet that all these species had cells as the engine that drove their life, receptors as buttons on a control panel, and peptides or other ligands that pushed those buttons—the receptors. A single neuron can support 200,000 junctions with other nerve cells. The neuron transmits information electronically and chemically—then as now.

I can't explain how our brains make decisions, nor can anyone else. I can imagine that our brain now is different than the brain of our ancestors, and that each of us has a different brain. All I need is an expert or scientist that can explain how the brain functions today, and then I hope that I can establish a biological defense or establish evidence that will justify mitigation of punishment if not a defense to the crime. Consider the following Tennessee case from the 1990s: Richard Odom.

IX

Neurobiological Mitigation Evidence:
Richard Odom
(Murder)

Our own genomes carry the story of evolution, written in DNA, the language of molecular genetics, and the narrative is unmistakable.

— Kenneth R. Miller

ALTHOUGH I BECAME INTERESTED in crime and genetics in the 1970s, I did not actually assert a biological defense until the 1990s. This was a death penalty case in Memphis, Tennessee, where the defendant Richard Odom (now still on death row) had been convicted of murder and the case reversed on appeal only for resentencing.

I was court-appointed, and I immediately began an investigation and concluded there was only one possible way to mitigate the punishment—life not death. I associated a young Memphis lawyer, Bob Brooks, to assist me and employed a person to investigate Odom's background in Mississippi. Odom had been living on the street in Memphis, Tennessee, but he had lived most of his life in Mississippi. *The Commercial Appeal*, a Memphis newspaper, reported the case as appears on the next pages.

Killer's confession to 1991 slaying is read to life-or-death jury

By Lawrence Buser
The Commercial Appeal

A 1991 murder case that later led to the ouster of former Tennessee Supreme Court Justice Penny White is back in court, where a new jury is being asked to decide on a life or death sentence for defendant Richard L. Odom.

Odom was convicted and sentenced to death seven years ago for the rape-murder of 77-year-old Mina Ethel Johnson, whose body was found in her car in a parking garage on Madison and Pauline.

The state Supreme Court in 1996 upheld the conviction but overturned Odom's death sentence, ruling that the crime did not meet the legal test of "heinous, atrocious and cruel" and that it was not among "the worst of the worst."

The decision was criticized by victims' rights groups across the state, and White, the only justice up for a yes-no retention vote, was turned out of office by angry voters several months later.

State prosecutors Jerry Harris and Amy Weirich are seeking the death penalty again for Odom. This time, however, they are limited by the high court to using only Odom's prior crimes of violence – a 1978 murder in Mississippi and 1991 robbery in Memphis – as aggravating circumstances or the death penalty.

Odom's defense is that neurobiologists say he has low levels of serotonin, a naturally occurring chemical in the brain that studies show plays a role in self-control.

"Our whole case will be scientific evidence on the state of his brain," said Ed Chandler, one of two court-appointed attorneys for Odom. "He is biologically incapable of controlling rage. I think the issue right now is why was she murdered."

The defense also is expected to detail Odom's background of adoption, abuse and run-ins with the law, including truancy, running away, larceny and auto theft. He spent part of his teen years in juvenile facilities.

In Odom's sentencing trial, which began Wednesday, jurors were told that Johnson as on her way to a doctor's appointment on the afternoon of May 10, 1991, when she was accosted in a medical center parking garage.

Dr. Jerry Francisco, recently retired county medical examiner, testified that Johnson was stabbed in the heart, the lung and the liver and had defensive wounds on her right hand. He said the 113-pound woman also was raped.

Johnson was former executive secretary with Lincoln American Life Insurance Co.

Odom, arrested three days later, confessed to the murder after police told him his fingerprint had been found on a seat belt buckle in the victim's car.

"She said something like 'Son, you know this ain't right' and I told her 'Lady, I'm not your son. If you want your son I'll give you your son and I crawled in the back seat," Odom said in one of two statements read to the jury. "I don't know if I stabbed her when I got in the back seat with her or when I got back in the front seat."

Defense lawyers said Odom also told officers he needed mental or psychological help.

Jurors on Wednesday also learned of Odom's conviction for the 1978 murder of Becky Roberts, 40, the manager of the Showtime Drive-In Theater in Pearl, Miss., where Odom did occasional cleaning work.

Odom told police they got into an argument over money on May 4, 1978, and that a fight began when she hit him with a flower pot. Odom said he hit her back, cut her with a knife and then shot her in the eye with a 22-caliber rifle when she grabbed for the barrel.

Killer can't control impulses, jury told

By Lawrence Buser
The Commercial Appeal

A twice-convicted killer facing a life-or-death sentence for the 1991 rape and murder of an elderly Memphis woman has a chemical imbalance that leaves him unable to control his violent impulses, a jury was told Thursday.

Richard L. Odom also was given up for adoption at age 3 by his natural parents and was physically and sexually abused as he grew up in Mississippi, defense witnesses said.

The testimony came on the second day of Odom's resentencing trial for the stabbing death of 77-year-old Mina Ethel Johnson, whose body was found in the back seat of her car May 10, 1991, in a parking garage at Madison and Pauline in the Medical Center area.

Prosecutors are seeking to return Odom to death row, citing his prior crimes of violence, including the 1978 murder of a Mississippi woman.

Defense attorneys are asking jurors to give Odom a sentence of life in prison, noting his troubled childhood and low levels of the inhibitory brain chemical serotonin.

"There is a link between low serotonin activity in the brain and deficient impulse control," said Dr. S. Paul Rossby, a molecular neurobiologist at Vanderbilt University.

"I would say he is not biologically capable of controlling rage, though low serotonin is not the cause of rage."

Prosecutors noted, however, that while on death row for four years, records show Odom worked well with others and rarely showed rage.

Odom was convicted and sent to death row in 1992 for Johnson's murder.

Four years later the state Supreme Court upheld the conviction, but awarded him a new sentencing trial, saying the murder did not meet the legal test of being heinous, atrocious and cruel. Three months later, following a campaign by victims' rights group across the state, Justice Penny White was ousted by voters.

Odom also is under a life sentene for a 1978 murder in Pearl, Miss., where he stabbed and shot to death Becky Roberts, 40, the manager of a drive-in theater where Odom did part-time work.

The trial before Criminal Court Judge Chris Craft resumes today.

To reach reporter Lawrence Buser, call 529-2385 or E-mail buser@gomemphis.com

Jury again rules Odom to die for rape-slaying

By Lawrence Buser
The Commercial Appeal

A jury rejected a brain-chemical defense Friday and returned convicted killer Richard L. Odom to death row in a case that had been a rallying point for victims' rights groups across the state.

The eight men and four women deliberated for three hours before giving Odom the maximum punishment for the 1991 rape and murder of 77-year-old Mina Ethel Johnson in a parking garage at Madison and Pauline.

While waiting for the jury, Odom, 39, told one of several courtroom deputies guarding him, "Smile. It brightens up the room." Odom showed no reaction when the death penalty was announced.

The Criminal Court jury found that his two prior crimes of violence, a 1978 murder and a 1991 robbery, outweighed any mitigating factors, which the defense said included a low level of serotonin, a brain chemical involved in controlling impulses.

Prosecutors Jerry Harris and Amy Weirich urged jurors to reject the defense and explanations for Odom's behavior as "total psycho-babble" and unfounded "leaps of faith." They said the murder was not impulsive, noting that he initiated the action, disposed of evidence and initially lied to investigators.

"There comes a point when a person is responsible for his actions," said Harris, who argued that Odom left both victims in "display" positions as if to boast of his crimes. "That gives you a real insight into who the real Richard Odom is. That's his handiwork. Those are his signatures."

Over defense objections, Weirich repeatedly pointed to Odom and called him "that cold, manipulative, violent killer."

Defense attorneys Ed Chandler and Robert Brooks said Odom had a disrupted childhood and also contended that low levels of serotonin left Odom biologically unable to control his rage.

"It's not his fault that his brakes failed," said Chandler, who called Odom "a bad seed" and acknowledged that the murders were brutal. "If you're not mad at my client, then you're not human. You don't have to like him, but if you're going to be fair to him then use logic reason, science and the law."

Odom was convicted and sentenced to death in 1992 for Johnson's murder, but the state Supreme Court four years later awarded him a new sentencing trial, saying the murder did not qualify for the aggravating circumstance of being "heinous, atrocious and cruel."

Justice Penny White, the only member up for a yes-no retention vote, was voted out of office several months later in a voter backlash led by victims' rights groups who felt she was anti-death penalty and soft on crime.

In the new sentences trial, prosecutors relied only on the aggravating factor regarding prior crimes of violence.

In 1978, Odom was convicted and sentenced to life for the murder of Becky Roberts, 40, the manager of a drive-in theater in Pearl, Miss., where Odom worked part-time. She was beaten, stabbed and shot.

While serving his sentence, Odom walked away from a Simpson County, Miss., jail in 1991 and hitchhiked to Memphis, where he lived on the streets and got by robbing women of their purses.

Two months after he arrived, he attacked Johnson in the medical center parking garage, where he raped her and stabbed her to death in the back of her car.

A juror from Odom's 1992 conviction and death sentence said Friday she was "outraged" that a new panel of jurors had to hear the gruesome details and view graphic photos of the murder.

"This has upset me all over again that another jury has to go through the trauma, fear and anger that we did," said Brenda Gaston. "he raped and brutally murdered that little old lady on the floorboard of her car. She was a little bitty delicate flower. He (Odom) was sentenced to death, not to be put on death row. He should have been electrocuted."

To reach reporter Lawrence Buser, call 529-2385 or E-mail buser@gomemphis.com

Richard I. Odom was born Aug. 13, 1960, in Meadowville, Miss., and was adopted by family friends when his parents separated. He spent time in training schools as a teenager and had a history of juvenile problems including truancy, running away, larceny and auto theft.

One psychologist predicted in 1976 that Odom would be "a liability to society for the rest of his life."

Here is a timeline of Odom's criminal past and its effect on the makeup of the Tennessee Supreme Court:

May 1978: Kills acquaintance Becky Roberts, 40, the manager of a Pearl, Miss., drive-in where he worked part-time. She was beaten, shot and stabbed.

December 1978: Pleads guilty to first-degree murder to avoid death penalty, telling judge "I done the crime." Sentenced to life in prison.

July 1981: Escapes from Mississippi prison, but is recaptured two days later.

September 1990: Is transferred from South Mississippi Correctional Center in Greene County to the Simpson Country jail where he is made a cook.

March 1991: With trusty status in the jail, Odom takes out the trash and does not return.

April 1991: Is charged in Memphis with fraudulent use of a credit card and serves 12 days in Shelby County jail under the alias Otis Smith. Once released, Odom finds shelter in a vacant motel on Lamar near Prescott.

May 1991: Robs woman of her purse at knifepoint in Memphis.

May 1991: Two days later, rapes and stabs to death Mina Ethel Johnson, 77, in her car in a parking garage at Madison and Pauline. Fingerprints on her car match those on file from Odom's credit card arrest. With his police mug shot available, Odom is arrested three days later a few blocks from the crime scene. He confesses to the murder.

January 1992: Is sentenced to six years in prison for the purse robbery; prosecutors to use conviction as aggravating factor (a prior crime of violence) in death-penalty case.

October 1992: Is convicted of raping and murdering Johnson and sentenced to death by a Criminal Court jury.

July 1995: A federal magistrate in Mississippi allows Odom to withdraw his 1978 guilty plea to Roberts murder because of ineffective assistance of counsel.

June 1995: Tennessee Supreme Court upholds Odom's murder conviction, but rejects his death sentence, ruling in part that the Johnson murder did not meet the legal definition of "heinous, atrocious and cruel" and was not among "the worst of the worst."

August 1996: Seen as soft on crime, for her vote in the Odom case, Justice Penny White, the only court member up for yes-no retention vote, is removed from the bench by voters.

July 1998: In a new trial in the 1978 Mississippi murder, Odom again is convicted of killing Becky Roberts and again is sentenced to life in prison.

August 1998: Justice Adolpho Birch, who authored the opinion that overturned Odom's Tennessee death sentence, retains his seat despite victims' rights groups opposition.

September 1999: Odom's resentencing trial begins with Shelby County prosecutor again seeking the death penalty based on prior crime violence. Defense attorney seek a life sentence, says chemical imbalance leaves Odom unable to control violent impulses.

• *Lawrence B.*

Judge orders death sentence to run consecutive to life term

By Lawrence Buser
busier@commercialappeal.com

In a ruling that seemingly only a lawyer or judge could appreciate, a 46-year-old man sentenced for murders in two states will serve his Tennessee death sentence consecutive to his Mississippi life sentence.

The decision by Criminal Court Judge Chris Craft on Monday is to keep defendant Richard L. Odom from receiving ongoing prison credit for his life sentence while awaiting execution on the other.

Craft said he made the ruling in the event the death sentence is later commuted or reduced to life.

"It might sound silly to a lay person," Craft said of the life-and-death sentencing issue, "but a life sentence did not stop him in Mississippi." In both states, inmates can be released after serving a portion of a life sentence.

Odom, 46, was convicted of raping and murdering 77-year-old Mina Ethel Johnson on May 10, 1991, in a Medical Center parking garage at Madison and Pauline. He was arrested three days later, identified by fingerprints from the crime scene, and he confessed to the murder.

He had been in Memphis about six weeks after walking away from the Simpson County Jail in Mendenhall, Miss., where he was a trusty serving a life sentence for the 1978 murder of Becky Roberts, 40, the manager of a drive-in theater in Pearl.

Odom was convicted of Johnson's murder in 1992 and was sentenced to death by three separate juries – the third jury's verdict was last month – after the first two death sentences were over-turned by the Tennessee Supreme Court.

Craft said that because the murder occurred before 1999 when lethal injection became the method of execution in Tennessee, Odom also has the option of choosing electrocution.

No execution date has been set, though appeals are expected to take years.

Lawrence Buser: 529-2385

Sentence: Death

The defendant was thus sentenced to death again at the second sentencing hearing. We appealed. The Tennessee Court of Criminal Appeals affirmed, but the Tennessee Supreme Court reversed and remanded for a third sentencing hearing before another new jury. On appeal, the Tennessee Court of Criminal Appeals had summarized the proof as follows:

Glori Shettles Johnson, a private investigator whose work mostly involved capital cases for defense attorneys, testified that she obtained personal records and a social history of the defendant's childhood. Her research established that the defendant's biological parents, Richard Norman Smith and Nellie Ruth Holley Henry, married in 1958 when Mr. Smith was 18 years old and Ms. Henry was 15. The defendant was born in Mississippi on August 13, 1960, and was named Richard Lloyd Smith. He had an older sister, born in 1959, and a younger sister, born in 1962.

The defendant lived with his parents until they abandoned him at the age of two and a half. The defendant never saw his mother again and did not see his father again except for a brief encounter when he was 13. The defendant's father reported that he drank heavily as a young man and was often away from home. He said that the defendant's mother was young, did not want the children, and did not care for them properly. The defendant's parents often fought and left the children at a day care center in Jackson, Mississippi, "for days at a time." Shirley and Jimmy Odom lived near the day care center and adopted the defendant in 1963. Other members of the Odom family adopted the defendant's sisters.

The Odoms already had three children of their own, Cindy, Larry, and Jimmy, when they adopted the defendant. The defendant's adoptive father was not physically abusive but was "very stern" and "very loud." By the time the defendant was five years old, the Odoms had divorced and Mrs. Odom had remarried. She married Marvin Bruce, and they had three children of their own. Mr. Bruce was "mean" and "cruel to the children." Mr. Bruce sexually abused the defendant and Larry Odom and threatened to kill them and their mother if they told anyone about the abuse.

The defendant's adoptive grandmother never accepted the defendant and was "very, very physically abusive" to him. The grandmother once whipped the defendant "so much that her son had to literally pull her off because he was afraid of what she was doing." Many reports also surfaced of the defendant being burned with cigarettes on his feet, but Johnson was unable to verify this with medical documentation. Family members reported that the defendant was always hungry, and Marvin Bruce often gave the defendant his food after deliberately putting hot sauce on it and in the defendant's mouth.

The defendant also wet his bed from the time he came into the Odom home until his early teens. Mr. Bruce berated the defendant for this, saying, "Why are you doing this, why can't you grow up, why can't you be a man[?]" The defendant also had a problem with sleepwalking and once, while sleepwalking, urinated in Mr. Bruce's car and in the refrigerator on more than one occasion.

The defendant did not learn he was adopted until he was about 12 years old. He began running away from home and was charged with larceny in the juvenile system at age 13. He was institutionalized at the Columbia Training School at age 13 and was evaluated by a psychologist, Dr. Cox, who described the defendant as "[s]chizoid" and opined that he was "incorrigible . . . brain damaged . . . not fit for society at age thirteen." Two years later, as the defendant continued to have problems in the juvenile system, Dr. Cox evaluated him again, finding that he "caused a lot of his own problem[s] and that he would probably be destined for a life of institutionalization." At age 16, the defendant was placed on juvenile parole and released into the community.

During cross-examination, Johnson said that further research revealed that the defendant's adoptive brother, Larry Odom, had a criminal record and was incarcerated for approximately ten years. She believed that the defendant's other adoptive brother, Jimmy Odom, had a juvenile record but was unable to verify it. No reports of any of the Bruce children having a criminal history surfaced during Johnson's investigation.

While imprisoned in Mississippi for his conviction for the murder of Becky Roberts, the defendant had behaved well enough to be transferred from Parchman State Penitentiary to the South Mississippi Correctional Center in Green County and then to the Simpson County Jail, where he was a trustee. Since being incarcerated in the Tennessee Department of Correction, the defendant had received a correspondence paralegal degree from the Professional Career Development Institute, scoring 100% in criminal law and between 90 and 100% in each of the other legal areas. The defendant also had received good reports from the Department of Correction, indicating that he was not having difficulties in prison and had been able to conform his behavior to the mandates of the prison.

Dr. Dennis Earl Schmidt, a neuropharmacologist and neurochemist at Vanderbilt University School of Medicine, testified that he, Dr. Steven Rossby, and Dr. Benjamin Johnson performed a spinal tap on the defendant in prison during the summer of 1999. Dr. Johnson actually performed the procedure, withdrawing six one-milliliter samples of fluid from the defendant's spinal canal. Dr. Schmidt carried the samples to his laboratory at Vanderbilt for analysis. Each sample of cerebrospinal fluid was analyzed in triplicate using a technique called "high-performance liquid chromatography," which utilizes a machine to separate and quantitate the amount of the different components of the fluid. The results of the analysis revealed that the defendant had very low levels of serotonin in his brain, less than half of normal levels. Dr. Schmidt provided the results of his analysis in writing to Dr. Rossby.

Dr. Steven Paul Rossby, a molecular neurobiologist and a professor at Vanderbilt University School of Medicine, testified that he statistically analyzed Dr. Schmidt's results and concluded that the defendant's serotonin function was "severely, extremely abnormal . . . the lowest level we've ever seen in our lab." Dr. Rossby explained that brain chemistry research performed on inmates in Finland and Sweden showed a very strong link between low serotonin and impulsive behavior, including unrestrained aggression, violence, and rage. However, the research did not indicate that low serotonin makes a person aggressive but did indicate low self-control. The impulses released by the low self-control depends on individual factors, such as heredity and early childhood experiences. Dr. Rossby opined that if a person has a low serotonin level, "any kind of excitatory stimulus or trigger or occurrence would not be as controlled as a normal person. The capacity to control these impulsive behaviors is diminished by low serotonin."

Dr. Rossby testified that the defendant's control of anger could "rapidly be lost," triggering rage which could "rapidly escalate into full-blown rage," as a result of his serotonin level. When questioned about the victim using the word "son" when the defendant attacked her, Dr. Rossby related:

> The use of the word "son," . . . in my expert opinion, could have served as trigger to release the rage that he felt toward his mother or mother figures or any women who were in his life in a mother capacity who didn't protect him or who rejected him. The word "son" could function as a trigger to cause an ensemble of neurons to fire, resulting in a rage reaction which is not effectively opposed by his serotonin levels and essentially is discontrolled.

> But I'm not saying that's what happened. I'm saying that, based on what I've read and based on the scientific evidence, . . . that could explain -- biologically could explain how it escalated to the point that it did. And I also feel that the humiliating position that he placed [the

65

victim) in is also an expression of rage. And in reading his life history and learning that he was abandoned around two years old and then the succession of circumstances in his life, I think it's quite plausible that his control mechanisms did not develop normally.

On cross-examination, Dr. Rossby admitted that he was a doctor of philosophy, not a medical doctor, and that he was being paid $150 per hour for his time in court and $100 per hour for his time out of court. He conceded that no studies exist to support that low serotonin causes violent behavior, and could not say that the defendant's low serotonin caused him to murder Becky Roberts or rape and murder the victim.

In rebuttal, the State presented Dr. John Robert Hutson, a clinical psychologist, who also testified regarding serotonin:

You can't say that serotonin causes anything. .... There seems to be a relationship between serotonin – and we don't even know very much about, as I understand it, what levels and what emotional states, let alone, anything about what behaviors. But what that relationship is, whether it is a causal one, that's – I don't know anyone that knows that at this point.

Serotonin: Prosecutors Rebuttal Evidence

Dr. Hutson said he was not aware of any literature indicating a causal effect between serotonin and violent behavior, obesity, depression, or suicide attempts. (See opinion next page.) On cross-examination, Dr. Hutson admitted that this was the first time he had testified specifically on the subject of serotonin. Would he not be surprised at the literature and scientific studies since he testified? There has been literature since the 1990s supporting my theory (contrary to Dr. Hudson's testimony, his opinions).

Tennessee Supreme Court: Second Sentencing Hearing

From the Supreme Court opinion reversing and remanding for resentencing:

66

Dr. Rossby, a molecular neurobiologist, testified that Dr. Schmidt's test results indicated that the defendant's serotonin level was "severely, extremely abnormal" and the lowest level ever seen at his lab. Citing studies conducted in Finland and Sweden, Dr. Rossby explained that low serotonin levels are very strongly linked to "impulsive behaviors[,] includ[ing] unrestrained aggression, violence, [and] rage." Although Dr. Rossby stated that low serotonin levels could cause a person to exhibit low self-control of impulses, he explained that "whatever impulses that are released by this low self-control depends upon the individual, depends on their birth, depends on their heredity, depends on their early childhood experiences." He testified that the victim's use of the word "son" may have "served as a trigger to release the rage that [the defendant] felt toward his mother or mother figures . . . ."

Dr. Rossby conceded that low serotonin levels have also been associated with nonviolent behaviors such as eating disorders and gambling addiction. In addition, he admitted that there were no studies conclusively linking low serotonin levels to violent behavior and that he could not state that the defendant's low serotonin level caused him to commit the murder of Mina Ethel Johnson. Although the defendant had no problems controlling impulsive rage while in prison, Dr. Rossby stated that the ability to control impulses is not tested as often in the structured environment of prison.

Prosecution's Rebuttal Evidence

In rebuttal, the prosecution presented the testimony of Dr. John Hutson, a clinical psychologist. Although Dr. Hutson testified that he was quite impressed with Dr. Rossby's testimony as a whole, he opined that based upon the current scientific understanding of the role of serotonin, it cannot really be said that "that serotonin causes anything." In addition, Dr. Hutson testified that he was not aware of any literature stating that there is a causal relationship between serotonin, violent behavior, obesity, depression, suicide, or other abnormal behaviors.

At the conclusion of the sentencing proceeding, the jury determined that the evidence of the single aggravating circumstance outweighed the evidence of mitigating circumstances beyond a reasonable doubt and sentenced the defendant to death for the felony murder of Mina Ethel Johnson. After the Court of Criminal Appeals affirmed the sentence, the case was docketed automatically before this Court.

Tennessee Supreme Court: Third Sentence Hearing

I prepared a defense for another sentencing hearing based upon the amygdala (which is comprised of a set of two small masses of gray matter inside each cerebral hemisphere that are involved with the experiencing of emotions) and low serotonin as mitigation evidence. In my mind, I would have to find another (or two) experts to support Dr. Rossby's testimony. I could do a better job. But my client did not want another biological defense! I withdrew. (I could have improved the mitigation evidence.)

Marty B. McAfee and Gerald Skahan were appointed to represent Richard Odom at the third hearing. Richard Odom was again sentenced to death. This sentence was affirmed by the Tennessee Court of Appeals, No. W2008-0246-CCA-R3-PD, and the Tennessee Supreme Court affirmed. No. W2008-02464-SC-DOT-DD (2011). The sentence of death was to be carried out March 13, 2012.

Tennessee Supreme Court: Third Sentencing Hearing Appeal

The proof (in part) summarized by the Tennessee Supreme Court (third appeal) in its opinion:

> With this standard in mind, we must address the weighing of the aggravating and mitigating circumstances. The State proved that the Defendant had murdered Becky Roberts in 1978. The jury was presented with the judgment of conviction for that crime. The State also presented evidence that the Defendant murdered the victim in this case during a robbery. The State submitted photographic and testimonial evidence describing the nature and circumstances of the crime, which allowed the jury to assess the weight to be given the proffered aggravating circumstances.
>
> In mitigation, the defense presented the Defendant's personal history, which outlined his abandonment by his birth parents and separation from his siblings at a young age. It illustrated the abusive home life the Defendant experienced as a result of his adoptive mother's remarriage, the emotional rejection he experienced as a child, and his involvement with juvenile authorities in Mississippi. The defense described his stay at the Columbia Training Center, where two psychological evaluations identified the Defendant's need for psychological treatment, which he never received. The jury also heard evidence

concerning the Defendant's almost spotless record while incarcerated at Riverbend, where he received his GED and a paralegal certification, worked as a teacher's aide, participated in a variety of classes, and engaged in arts and crafts. Several parties who had come into contact with the Defendant during his incarceration testified to the Defendant's efforts at self-improvement and his capacity for rehabilitation in a structured prison environment. The jury also heard from Dr. Joseph Angelillo, who believed the Defendant suffered from "schizoid personality features" and opined that the Defendant had the capacity to do well in the prison environment. The State rebutted this evidence by describing the Defendant's escape from prison and his prior theft and robbery convictions, both of which were committed after his escape.

While the defense offered extensive proof of circumstances in mitigation of the crime, the two aggravating circumstances were firmly established by the evidence. The State also presented evidence that the jury could have used to assess the weight to be given the aggravating and mitigating circumstances. As a result, there was a sound basis for the jury's determination that the aggravating circumstances outweighed the mitigating ones beyond a reasonable doubt.

The defendant was still on "death row" in 2017. This third sentencing hearing failed as well as our second. (I was not surprised.)

X

The Theory of the Neurobiological Amygdala Defense and Mitigation Evidence

There is a time for some things, and a time for all things; a time for great things, and a time for small things.

— Miguel de Cervantes Saavedra,
Don Quixote de la Mancha

THE AMYGDALA DEFENSE

MAKE TWO FISTS with your hands, tucking the thumbs under your fingers. Hold one fist to each side of your head with the heel of the hand pressed to the temple. The fists represent the temporal lobes, the lateral boundary of the limbic system.

Now remove your fists. Turn them over so that the fingers are face up as if the brain has been removed from the skull and flipped over. The tips of your thumbs show the approximate size, shape, and position of each of two amygdaloid nuclei or "amygdalae."[14] The space below the joint at the base of each thumb represents the hippocampus curving inward to slot the amygdala into place between

---

14 "Amygdale" is the Greek word for almond, and the amygdala is named so because of a portion which is almond shaped. The amygdala has twelve distinct divisions and is located on each side of the brain in the tissue. (The *Batman* comic series "Shadow of the Bat" features a monster called "Amygdala" who was named after this almond-shaped mass of nerves in the brain that control, among other things, feelings of rage.)

the lateral edges of the hypothalamus and the overlying temporal cortex.

According to Joseph E. LeDoux, a leading authority in the field of neural science, the amygdala can be "provoked into expressing unconsciously controlled emotional responses." The amygdala could unconsciously commit a crime that the conscious person would never condone. This is not a "crime of passion" in which a law-abiding and reasonable person commits a crime during a lapse of rationality or sanity, nor is it a pathological brain defense which is based upon a physical alteration in the brain. The rationale is neurological. The amygdala defense is based upon the notion that the amygdala controls emotional behavior in an unconscious, Pavlovian manner; the crime is committed independent of conscious thought. The amygdala controls an aggressive act independent of conscious control in provocative circumstances (Brockman, 2002).[15]

Note the criteria for the defense in order for the defense to be established:

---

15 In *The Next Fifty Years* (2002), Dr. Joseph LeDoux, Professor of Science, Center for Neural Science, New York University, explains in detail the amygdala defense and the function of the amygdala. See also "Taming Stress," by Dr. Robert Sapolsky, *Scientific American*, September 2003, and his explanation of the amygdala and the activation of the amygdala and the sympathetic nervous system from implicit memory that does not require "conscious awareness." See "Dysfunction in the Neural Circuitry of Emotion Regulation – A possible Prelude to Violence," by Davidson, Putnam, & Larson, *Science*, July 28, 2000 [Appendix p. 38]; "Searching for the Mark of Cain," by Martin Enserink, *Science*, July 28, 2000 [Appendix p. 37]; "High Anxiety," by Goldman, *Science*, November 29, 1996 [Appendix p. 77]; "Enhanced aggressive behavior in mice lacking 5-HT1B receptor," by Saudou et al., *Science,* September 23, 1994; "Convergent Pathways for Steroid Hormone- and Neurotransmitter-Induced Rat Sexual Behavior," by Mani, Allen, Clark, Blaustein, & O'Malley, *Science*, August 26, 1994; and "Neural Feel for Seeing," by Bruce Bower, *Science News*, November 23, 2004.

1. The crime involves a relatively simple, innate, stereotyped response;
2. executed instantaneously; and
3. without premeditation upon the occurrence of the provocation.

According to Davidson, Putnam, and Larson, in a paper titled "Dysfunction in the neural circuitry of emotion regulation—A possible prelude to violence,"

Emotion is normally regulated in the human brain by a complex circuit consisting of the orbital frontal cortex, amygdala, anterior cingulate cortex, and several other interconnected regions. There are both genetic and environmental contributions to the structure and function of this circuitry.

We posit that impulsive aggression and violence arise as a consequence of faulty emotion regulation. Indeed, the prefrontal cortex receives a major serotonergic projection, which is dysfunctional in individuals who show impulsive violence. Individuals vulnerable to faulty regulation of negative emotion are at risk for violence and aggression. (2000)

In the future, we should know more about the balance between conscious and unconscious control in the brain.[16]

---

16 The major unsolved problem in biology is explaining "how billions of neurons swapping chemicals give rise to such subjective experiences as consciousness, self-awareness, and awareness that others are conscious and self-aware." See Blackmore, *Consciousness: An Introduction* (2010).

THE AMYGDALA AND THE LIMBIC SYSTEM

It's not your circumstances that shape you, it's how you react to your circumstances.

— Anne Ortlund, best-selling women's author

All emotional experiences result from the activation of the limbic system. The limbic system's main components are the hippocampus, the cingulate gyrus, and the amygdala. The limbic system communicates with the cerebral cortex. Emotions may be triggered without knowledge of the cortex; the amygdala reacts without benefit of input from the cortex. According to Dr. LeDoux, "emotional responses can occur without the involvement of the higher processing systems of the brain, systems involved in thinking, reasoning, and consciousness." In his book *Synaptic Self: How Our Brains Become Who We Are*, he says:

> The amygdala detects danger by virtue of its position in a synaptically connected system. In its simplest form, this system can be described in terms of a three-level excitatory chain of cells that releases glutamate—projection cells in sensory systems activate projection cells in the amygdala, which activate projection cells in motor control areas.
>
> Amygdala cells receive inputs from the sensory world constantly, but they ignore the majority of them.... They do get worked up, though, when the right stimulus is present—one that signifies danger or some other biologically significant event....
>
> In the amygdala,...[the resting membrane potential of] some cells can be as negative as minus 80 millivolts, due to sustained or toxic inhibition by the amino acid GABA. With GABA receptors on amygdala projection

cells occupied and passing chloride, the inside of the cells becomes more negative, which means it takes extra excitation to turn the amygdala on.... The stimulus has to have special qualities that allow it to overcome the tonic inhibition produced by GABA.

Stimuli that are inherently dangerous (the sight or smell of a predator) or unpleasant (intense stimuli, like loud noises or stimuli that cause pain) are able to overcome the tonic inhibition, as are stimuli that have emotional resonance acquired through past learning.... Both innate (hardwired) and learned danger signals cause amygdala cells to fire rapidly for a sustained period and are thus able to overcome the GABA guard. (1998, pp. 61-63)

An otherwise meaningless sound of modest intensity that previously occurred in association with pain has the same effect as a natural (innate) form of danger.

There are two different paths to the amygdala. One leads directly from the thalamus; the other, from the periphery, to the thalamus, to the cortex, to the amygdala. The cortical path allows for elaboration and meaning. It takes 12 milliseconds for a sound to reach the amygdala via the thalamus. It takes almost 24 milliseconds via the path through the cortex! For example, we react to gunfire by diving for cover—before we know what's happening. Our sensory cortex provides an explanation later. Conscious recognition is after the anxiety, which was generated unconsciously. The anxiety began milliseconds before conscious recognition.

The amygdala can appraise and respond to a situation an instant before the cortex provides an explanation. This may be a reason why psychotherapy is rarely successful in the treatment of phobia or any of the other five major anxiety disorders.

Post-traumatic stress disorder (PTSD) is an anxiety

disorder, for example, which involves reliving vivid and emotionally wrenching memories of a horrifying experience. A person living with PTSD may startle in response to simply a loud noise. To a war veteran, a door slamming may activate a full-fledged stress response, causing him to dive for cover or break out in a sweat. Blood pressure and pulse may rise. His hypothalamus goes into gear, activating endocrine organs which release stress-related hormones into the blood system. There is a sense of vulnerability and helplessness.

These symptoms cannot be willed away. No preventative measures are possible. Trauma biases the brain such that the thalamic path to the amygdala overrides the cortical. These processing networks take the lead in the learning and storage of information. In panic attacks, internal rather than external events act as triggers. Blood flow changes in the temporal lobe, hippocampus, and amygdala. The attack activates the amygdala and its projections to the sympathetic nervous system, which is responsible for the body's "fight-or-flight" response. Uncertainty and anxiety build and explode in a full-blown panic attack.

We are all different. Genetic and temperamental variables play a role in anxiety. Fear-conditioned infants show strikingly different temperaments. Some respond to new situations with agitated movements of arms and legs, fretting, and crying outbursts. Others respond hardly at all.

The tendency to develop anxiety appears to run in families. Anxious parents tend to produce anxious children. Genetic or environment? Once an anxious temperament becomes established, it leads to anxiety even in situations lacking a reasonable basis for anxiety.

The brain is organized such that certain areas handle specific emotions. Damage to the left hemisphere often results in symptoms of depression such as crying, agitation, and expressions of hopelessness. Damage to the right hemisphere often induces an inappropriate cheerfulness and a tendency to make light of the damaging effects of the injuries or even deny them altogether.

The left prefrontal cortex is involved in positive emotions. The right deals with negative emotions. The prefrontal cortex, particularly the left prefrontal cortex, may be important in dampening the response to negative events and in shutting off a negative response quickly once it has been activated. The left prefrontal areas may accomplish this by inhibiting the amygdala.

Balance between the prefrontal cortex and the amygdala is important. Anxiety protects many of us from reckless behavior, impulsive decisions—even crime. We anxiously imagine ourselves in prison or otherwise deprived of freedom, reputation, or possessions.

But in prison, criminals with frontal-lobe impairment fail to learn from negative experiences of forced confinement. They are not uncomfortable. They lack normal, appropriate anxiety. After release, the prospect of future incarceration does not induce the necessary anxiety to avoid crime.

Hardened criminals often describe a lack of anxiety about the danger of a criminal career. Their failure to experience basic human emotions, whatever the cause, gets them into more crime. They do not experience fear or anxiety. They lose their ability to feel emotions relative to future consequences of their actions.

Neurotransmitters are among the smallest of the ligands. Several are composed of just one amino acid (for example glycerine). These tiny chemical molecules send specific messages across the synapse. Different combinations of neurotransmitters, each of which can exhibit different states (such as weak versus strong), result in different behaviors, thoughts, and emotions. The neurotransmitters of emotion are norepinephrine, serotonin, and dopamine. These play roles in mood and behavior.

The autonomic nervous system consists of the

sympathetic division and the parasympathetic division. The first organizes the body's responses to events that require maximum exertion—the "fight-or-flight" response. The parasympathetic oversees the "relax and smell the flowers" approach called the relaxation response. Both connect the central nervous system with the smooth muscle of internal organs, blood, and skin.

In John Brockman's *The Next Fifty Years*, Dr. LeDoux states that the amygdala defense should not be confused with the "pathological brain defense," which is based upon physical alteration of the brain. The amygdala defense is based upon the notion that the amygdala controls emotional behavior. He believes that the amygdala defense can be asserted today in relatively few cases but that in the next fifty years, discoveries about the balance between conscious and unconscious control may result in reconsidering our definition of human responsibility for crime. Why not the next ten years? Why not now?

Fifty years from now, the amygdala defense will be a reality. Today it's in its infancy, ready to be asserted in the right case by a defense lawyer who understands neurobiology and can hire experts that have the qualifications to describe the amygdala and its role in some crimes. Suppose you have no other defense? Can you find the expert?

> *"Give your evidence," said the King, "and don't be nervous, or I'll have you executed on the spot."*
> — Lewis Carroll, *Alice's Adventures in Wonderland*

Most lawyers and judges have been brainwashed by religious theories of "free will" and will consciously or subconsciously have a difficult time with the presentation of scientific or neurobiological defenses. Novel defenses such as the "amygdala defense" are particularly troublesome.

Ignorance, bias, and dishonesty of jurors must also be overcome, but first the criminal defense lawyer must understand the defense. It is a difficult defense to assert in this day and time.

Biology is to crime
as physics is to baseball.

This is a beginning point. Humans are biological animals. I'll repeat again. We arose from simple organisms to multicellular organisms over millions of years. Our bodies are composed of cells, 100 trillion per human. These cells are factories that manufacture 50,000 different proteins from 20 different amino acids. We had a common ape ancestor with the chimpanzee. Our brains are similar. Our DNA is 98.4 percent identical. Chimpanzees and other descendants of the ape have a limbic system with hippocampus, cingulate gyrus, and amygdala just like ours.

MITIGATION EVIDENCE:
AMYGDALA, LIMBIC SYSTEM, AND SEROTONIN

If the convicted defendant suffered from low levels of the neurotransmitter serotonin, to mitigate punishment (i.e., avoid the death penalty), neurobiological evidence can be introduced to establish how life experiences or relevant memories were colored by the amygdala—resulting in conscious, impulsive, criminal behavior.

In mitigation, at the second sentencing hearing in the case of Richard Odom, Dr. Rossby, a Vanderbilt University molecular neurobiologist, testified that in his opinion Richard Odom was biologically incapable of controlling his rage due to a low level of the neurotransmitter serotonin. He based his opinion on a spinal tap[17] and scientific analysis by Dr. Schmitt, a Vanderbilt University neuropharmacologist (who also testified) that the samples of cerebrospinal fluid had a mean concentration (from 18 different laboratory tests) of an acid (identified as 5HIAA) of 62.4 nanograms per milliliter.

Dr. Rossby's scientific research had established the average for a carefully controlled male group as 174.57 (ng/ml), which was the lowest level of serotonin he had ever professionally experienced. His opinion was also based upon 30 years of scientific research and experimentation reported in scientific literature. The state offered no expert evidence contra.

The "trigger" for the 1991 murder of Ms. Johnson was calling Richard "son." The "trigger" for the 1978 murder of Ms. Roberts was the attempt to hit him with a flower pot in the argument. Stored in Richard's memory and colored by his amygdala were bitter childhood experiences involving his mother, as he had been abandoned by her, adopted, and abused as a child.

What do children remember?

Memory has three components: acquisition, storage (learning), and retrieval (recall). Memories are stored as changes in the number and strength of the connections between neurons called synapses. A typical brain cell makes thousands of synapses with other neurons, but only some of those are involved in a particular memory. Genes are responsible for parts of the memory creation process.

---

17 A lumbar puncture is performed by inserting a needle between the third and fourth lumbar vertebrae (L3-L4) and withdrawing cerebrospinal fluid from the subarachnoid space. There is no possible injury of the spine. The cauda equine, which lies below L2, consists of the elongated spinal roots from the lumbar sacral spinal cord. A needle can also safely be inserted into the lumbar cistern at L2. The needle slips between the spinal roots. There is no danger of penetrating the spinal cord.

Conscious memory for facts and the emotional memory are two different systems.

Memory is a brain function divided into long-term and short-term. Short-term memory is used, for instance, when you commit a telephone number to memory just long enough to dial it, and then it is lost. All memory traces begin as short-term memories. Those committed to long-term storage are linked by emotion, by association, and by repetition to the overall construct of memorial material.

Several areas of the brain are simultaneously involved in the establishment of a memory, its functional linkage to associated memories (and emotions), its consolidation in long-term memory storage, and its retrieval from storage in the form of a recollection. The brain's limbic system and hippocampus with its associated cortex, particularly temporal cortex, are crucial to memory consolidation and retrieval. The mammillary bodies at the base of the brain are also involved in retrieval.

Another interesting book that can help us understand the way serotonin works is *Inside the Brain: Revolutionary Discoveries of How the Mind Works*, by Ronald Kotulak (1997). He explains that serotonin-producing cells in the midbrain send out as many as 500,000 connections to other cells by axons in every part of the brain. Serotonin keeps the peace with gentle, rhythmic pulses and allows our drives to live in harmony. Serotonin is the only neurotransmitter that sends out such connections, and the serotonin system is the largest single neurotransmitter system in the brain.[18] As of the time of publishing his book, sixteen different serotonin

---

18 Serotonin normally arrives in the frontal cortex by way of the raphe nucleus, a structure that also communicates with the locus coeruleus. Normally, serotonin stimulates the release of norepinephrine from the locus coeruleus. When serotonin becomes scarce, less norepinephrine is released – exacerbating the shortage caused by earlier unremitting glucocorticoid bombardment. (Sapolsky, 2003)

receptors have been found on brain cells.

Serotonin acts as a brake on impulses. Noradrenaline, the brain's alarm hormone, acts as an accelerator. But the ability to restrain aggression impulse control, the "braking power," depends on (1) environmental experiences and (2) genetic inheritance. Some people inherit a gene that makes them more susceptible to low serotonin. Early life experience (violent household, e.g.) determines how that gene will be expressed—whether serotonin levels will be set on low, normal, or high.

Low serotonin allows a person to be more impulsive. It is an adaptation to a threatening environment. The primitive drive of aggression goes unchecked. Normal serotonin levels are associated with clear thinking and social success. The risks are balanced against the benefits. These are the leaders and achievers. They are assertive and get things done. High levels of serotonin have the opposite effect of low levels. The brain "stops," and the person becomes afraid to do anything, like the deer that freezes when confronted by headlights or a wild animal confronted by its predator.

According to Kotulak, in humans, high serotonin levels are linked to the type of "fearfulness and rigidity of action as seen in obsessive-compulsive behavior." This anticipatory anxiety makes them feel that something bad is going to happen. Obsessive-compulsive persons have excessive activity in the front part of their brains. The ability to impose reason on their basic drives is knocked out.

In low serotonin cases with life histories of aggression, the opposite occurs—low brain activity. The brakes don't work. Regarding studies of criminal violence as related to serotonin, Kotulak reports, "When high noradrenaline was superimposed on low serotonin, impulsive aggression was aimed at others. When low noradrenaline was combined with low serotonin, aggression was aimed inward."

Sixty or more neurotransmitters have been identified

and named. Along with acetylcholine, dopamine, and norepinephrine, serotonin is among the most significant in terms of numbers and importance of the functions it helps carry out. The nerve cells that release and receive serotonin extend throughout the brain and down to the spinal cord.

In an article in the *Chicago Tribune*, "How Brain's Chemistry Unleashes Violence*,*" Kotulak described the finding of a study that was conducted in the late 1980s by Dr. Markku Linnoila, scientific director of the National Institute on Alcohol Abuse and Alcoholism, who found that

> the incidence of violence associated with low serotonin is impulsive, hot-blooded, involving a loss of control. This behavior characterizes irritable people who fly off the handle at the smallest challenge or perceived provocation—assaulting people, setting fires or committing violent suicides. (1993)

But Linnoila also offered hope for those who have low serotonin, whose lives are a storm of aggression. "Aggressive sociopaths tend to calm down in their forties—serotonin levels go up with age."

In her book, *Secrets of Serotonin: The Natural Hormone That Curbs Food and Alcohol Cravings, Reduces Pain, and Elevates Your Mood*, Carol Hart writes:

> The brain seems to function as a sort of democracy.... The multiple neurotransmitters and the different processing centers provide a system of checks and balances....
>
> One of serotonin's major roles is to modulate or control the effects of other...neurotransmitters, giving them a green, red, or yellow light...yet does not act alone. In the words of Thomas Carew, a Yale University research, "Serotonin is only one of the molecules in

the orchestra. But rather than being the trumpet or the cello player, it's the band leader who choreographs the output of the brain.".

Serotonin and other messenger molecules pass signals from one cell to another by interacting with special gatekeeper molecules called receptors...a lock-and-key system, in which each messenger molecule can unlock and activate only a specific receptor type. When a messenger molecule attaches to the proper receptor, the receptor triggers a series of responses within the cell, which may then release its own messengers to pass information onto yet other cells. Serotonin is known to unlock at least fifteen different receptor subtypes, each thought to have a distinct role in influencing some aspect of mood, functioning, and behavior. (2008, pp. 20-21)

Serotonin is known as 5-hydroxytryptamine (5-HT). It can be studied by analyzing the level of serotonin metabolite (its chemical breakdown product) in the spinal fluid, or other "markers" of serotonin in the blood. Serotonin is synthesized in different parts of the brain and body. (Ninety percent of serotonin in the body is in the "gut.") The most important raw ingredient is an amino acid called tryptophan.

Serotonin cannot pass from the bloodstream into the brain. It is prevented by the blood-brain barrier. The blood vessels in the brain have less permeable walls that control or limit the substances that can enter. Serotonin is too large a molecule to pass. According to Hart,

Another neurotransmitter called acetylcholine is generally believed to have the leading role in memory. However, serotonin may take the "best supporting role" nomination, with a strong secondary influence on our ability to learn and remember.... Serotonin syndrome is an emergency condition caused by an overdose of serotonin-active drugs. (pp. 34-39)

Serotonin abnormalities are inherited.[19] According to an article by Jocelyn Selim in *Discover Magazine*, December 2002, genes may control how scared we get:

Psychiatrist and neurologist Daniel Weinberger of the National Institute of Mental Health explored a long-suspected link between fear and a gene involved in regulating the brain's response to serotonin, a potent neurotransmitter. He and his team showed photographs of fearful faces to volunteers and then measured their reactions using MRI brain scans. People with a particular variant in the serotonin-control gene showed more activity in the amygdala, the emotional control center of the brain, and felt more anxious after seeing the photos. "Population-wide studies have already demonstrated that people with that variant are more likely to report fearfulness. Showing how that translates into brain activity makes the argument for a genetic influence pretty convincing," Weinberger says.

Genes may also mediate how we find our way out of our duress, says Beat Lutz of Germany's Max Planck Institute of Psychiatry. His team engineered mice whose brains cannot respond to naturally calming compounds called endocannabinoids. Lutz gave both engineered and normal mice an electric

---

19 A single gene defect is implicated in low serotonin. This gene "directs the production of a protein called tryptophan hydrolase, which converts tryptophan from such foods in the diet as wheat and other grains into serotonin. An error in the gene appears to make its possessor vulnerable to producing low serotonin, probably under stressful conditions, such as living in a violent family or drinking too much alcohol...." This requires a mutated serotonin-making gene and a stressor such as alcohol. (Kotulak, 1993)

shock, administered simultaneously with a loud tone, and then started playing only the tone. Normal mice soon became blasé when they heard the tone, but those lacking endocannabinoids worked themselves into a frenzy long after the shocks were over. "This could explain why some soldiers recover quickly, while others end up dealing with shell shock for decades," Lutz says. The finding may indicate that treatments aimed at boosting endocannabinoids could soothe the aftermath of bad experiences. (p. 14)

AMYGDALA DEFENSE FOR RICHARD ODOM

It wasn't until after sentencing in the Richard Odom case that I discovered the essay by Joseph LeDoux ("Mind, Brain, and Self") in the book *The Next Fifty Years* by John Brockman that set forth what I consider could have been a defense of "not guilty" for Richard Odom (before I became his defense lawyer) to the offenses themselves. Here's how he explained it:

The amygdala, like many brain regions, does its work outside our conscious awareness. We can become aware of the consequences of amygdala activation, but we do not have conscious access to its inner workings. Because the amygdala can be provoked into expressing unconsciously controlled emotional responses, the possibility is raised that the amygdala could unconsciously commit a crime—one that the conscious person would never willfully condone.

This possibility has not escaped lawyers. The legal system has long recognized "crimes of passion," in which an otherwise law-abiding and reasonable person commits a crime during a lapse of rationality or sanity. The "amygdala defense" adds a neurological rationale to this sort of argument. As we learn more about how the brain works, and lawyers learn more about what has been discovered, neurologically based defenses will become more and more common. So let's take a close look at what I mean by the amygdala defense.

First, the amygdala defense should not be confused with a related issue, which we can call the pathological brain defense. In the latter, the argument is that the person committed a crime because of some physical alteration in his or her brain. The amygdala defense, in contrast, is based on the notion that the amygdala normally controls emotional behavior in an unconscious fashion, and as a result it is possible for a crime to be committed by the amygdala independent of conscious thought. It is clearly possible for the amygdala to control an aggressive act independent of conscious control in certain provocative circumstances; however, in order for the amygdala defense to work, several criteria would have to be met.

An important job of the amygdala is to rapidly initiate protective responses in the face of sudden danger. But if the stimulus has been present for some time and consciously perceived, behavior tends to be under the control of higher thought processes, mediated by the cortex. Further, the kinds of responses directed by the amygdala are fast, simple, innate (hardwired) responses that are executed....

So if an act is deliberate, expressed relatively slowly (over seconds rather than milliseconds), involves a complex sequence of movements, and would be carried out differently in different people, it is probably not directly controlled by the amygdala. The amygdala can indirectly influence or modulate these more complex responses, but they are, in the end, the business of other brain systems. These facts suggest that in order for the amygdala defense to succeed, the crime would have to involve a relatively simple, innate, stereotyped response executed instantaneously and without premeditation upon the occurrence of the provocation.

I suspect that few crimes would meet the criteria necessary for the amygdala defense to succeed. However, it is becoming increasingly apparent that many brain systems other than the amygdala function unconsciously—and even that consciousness itself is the product of the unconscious workings of brain networks, raising the possibility that while the amygdala defense is wrong in name, it may still be valid in spirit. Whether we will need to reconsider the nature and limits of human responsibility, though, will depend on future discoveries about the balance between conscious and unconscious control in the brain. These, too, are likely to come in the next fifty years. (pp. 251-253)

XI

The World Tomorrow
Molecular Level and Beyond—The Future

*Science means constantly walking a tightrope
between blind faith and curiosity; between expertise
and creativity; between bias and openness; between
experience and epiphany; between ambition and
passion; and between arrogance and conviction—in
short, between an old today and a new tomorrow.*

— Heinrich Rohrer

NEURON CELLS have many variations in size, shape, and function. They almost always have an axon, a tail-like structure that is the biological equivalent of an electric cord. The axon may stretch across the brain or just a few centimeters. It splits into many branches, each of which lays up against the surface of a sister neuron.

Electrical charges generated in the cell body (DNA) are transmitted down the tail at a rate of one to sixty pulses per second. The aggregate of millions of pulses gives rise to the brain's electromagnetic aura and produces "brain waves" that can be captured by an electroencephalograph (EEG).

The purpose of the brain cells is to excite one another. The cells send and receive messages to one another. Many neurons have a set or sets of treelike antlers or "dendrites," branched protoplasmic extensions of the nerve cell that conduct impulses from adjacent cells toward the cell body (Pert, 349). At the level of molecules—big ones, little ones, medium-sized proteins, acids, fats—the molecules are linked.

Some of these molecules form the mitochondrion where chemical energy is produced. Other molecules change

88

the energy into electrical charges. Some form the cell's skeleton. Others compose the membrane that shields all the others from the outside world. Floating on the surface of the membranes are complex molecules called "receptors." The typical receptor is a large molecule consisting of hundreds of thousands of atoms. It floats on the cell's surface with its "roots" deep into the cell. These receptors are attached to the inner workings of the cells.

These receptors are more like a cup than a lily pad floating on the cell's surface. Some molecules can fit into the receptors. Others cannot. When another molecule "fits," it changes shape and sends a signal to the roots. The roots move and another cell is disturbed, then another, and another, etc. The reaction is in a domino fashion. The cell's metabolic rate increases. More electrical changes race down the axons, exciting other cells. This takes place in milliseconds. The individual human knows nothing and is totally unaware.

The key is the receptor. When molecules fit into the receptors, messages are carried. Receptors control the kidneys, the lungs, the heart, tell the intestines when to digest food, and so on. Receptors allow the immune system to recognize viruses and bacteria. Humans are colonies of cells, coordinated ecologies where various functions are controlled by a complex traffic of chemical messengers that carry this information in their shape and magnetic properties.

There is a tiny gap between the end of the axon ("bouton") and the receiving cell. Electricity, or the electrical impulse, jumps the gap, carrying a message by way of "neurotransmitters." The bouton releases a neurotransmitter that crosses the gap (or "synapse") to the surface of another cell. (The surface of a brain cell is covered with receptors.)

Mental illness results from damage or defects to such transmitter-receptor systems. Molecular psychologists study the chemical events that take place at the "synaptic cleft" between the bouton and the receiving neuron.

In May 1973, Candace Pert, working under Dr. Solomon Snyder (a neurochemist at Johns Hopkins Medical School, Baltimore, Maryland), conducted experiments and discovered for the first time receptors in brain cells. This was a scientific revolution, a beginning. Psychology had taken a giant step toward becoming a science.

All molecules of all substances are comprised of elements such as carbon, hydrogen, and nitrogen, which are bonded together in a configuration specific to that substance. This can be expressed as a chemical formula or drawn as a diagram. I predict that within fifty years, or "the world tomorrow," the cause of all serious crime will be expressed at the molecular level in such formulas or diagrams on a computer screen.

But life is controlled by molecules—the four bases of DNA. They spell out the message for inheritance in every creature that we know, from a bacterium to an elephant, from a virus to a rose.

Molecules are made of atoms. The atom has parts; it is not indivisible, as its Greek name (*atomos*, or "indivisible") implies. The electron is a tiny part of its mass or weight, but a real part, and it carries a single electric charge. In his book *The Ascent of Man*, Dr. Jacob Bronowski explains:

> Each element is characterized by the number of electrons in its atoms. And their number is exactly equal to the number of the place in Mendeleev's table that that element occupies when hydrogen and helium are included in first and second place. That is, lithium has three electrons, beryllium has four electrons, boron has five, and so on steadily all through the table.
>
> The place in the table that an element occupies is called its atomic number, and now that turned out to stand for a physical reality within its atom—the number of electrons there. The picture has shifted from atomic

90

weight to atomic number, and that means essentially to atomic structure.

AUTHOR'S NOTE

Obviously, neurobiological mitigation evidence could be used today to mitigate the punishment of Richard Odom from death to life. I failed. I believe if I could assert the defense theory today and with three or four new experts, I could "win." He now sits on death row in Nashville, Tennessee. Surely I could find one juror out of twelve that believes in evolution and would accept this biological defense.

XII

The Search for Truth
at the Molecular Level

*Science is the search for truth, that is the effort to
understand the world: it involves the rejection of
bias, of dogma, of revelation, but not the rejection of
morality.*

— Linus Pauling

A CELL is the smallest structural unit of an organism that is
capable of independent functioning, consisting of one or more
nuclei, cytoplasm, and various organelles, all surrounded by
a semipermeable cell membrane. Cell receptors are located
in this membrane, where they are available to bind with
various ligands suspended in the extracellular fluid that
bathes all cells and serves to transport the various nutrients,
waste products, and informational substances.

In her book, *Molecules of Emotion*, Candace Pert
(1999) defines the cortex as

> the outer layer of gray matter in the brain that covers the
> cerebral hemisphere. The frontal portion of the cortex
> is the most recently evolved of the brain structures
> and is present only in primates, such as ourselves. It
> contains neuronal centers necessary for understanding
> and producing language, for conceptualization and
> abstraction, for judgment, and for the capacity of
> humans to contemplate and exert control over their
> lives. (p. 349)

The brain contains 100 billion neurons (cells) and 600
glial cells. According to Pert,

Glial cells are any of the non-neuronal constituent cells of the brain or the peripheral nervous system...[and] are generally considered to support the functions of the neurons. A specialized immune cell derived from the monocyte is the microglial cell, which functions as part of the brain's immune system. The vast majority, some 90 percent, of the brain's cells are glia, not neurons. (p. 349)

The neuron consists of a body, one axon, and dendrite(s). It communicates via electricity. Recently, it has been discovered that glial cells also are involved in the decision-making process and are not just "glue." Just as no one knows how the decision-making process works, the glial cells are also a mystery.

All cells of the entire brain and body are composed of atoms. An atom is a unit of matter, the smallest unit of an element having all the characteristics of that element and consisting of a dense, central, positively charged nucleus surrounded by a system of electrons in defined regions in space called orbitals. There are 257 known sub-atomic particles. Molecules are comprised of atoms.

To understand atoms is to move from biology to physics. All matter is made up of molecules, and molecules are bound states of atoms. There are 92 different atoms in nature. The size of an atom (outer orbit of electrons) is 1/100,000,000 cm. The nucleus is 100,000 times smaller. The atom is mostly empty space! Imagine that the nucleus is a tennis ball, 6.35 cm in diameter. The nucleus contains protons and neutrons. The first electron circles at a distance of 6.35 km (4 miles).

The number of electrons in an atom is equal to the number of protons, and therefore atoms are electrically neutral. If an electron is knocked off an atom, it is no longer electrically neutral. It has a positive charge and is called an ion. The lowest mass atom is hydrogen—one electron in orbit with one proton in the nucleus. It has a size of 0.00000001 cm.

A proton contains three different types of "quarks." No structure of a quark (or an electron) has ever been observed. The proton, neutron, nucleus, and atom have sizes that can be measured. There are many other subatomic particles—257 or more. This discussion of elementary particle physics is limited, and further discussion is beyond the scope of my analysis.

Energy is a fundamental concept that plays a central role in elementary particle physics, also beyond the scope of this discussion.

There is a force, quite strong, that binds the neutrons and protons inside a nucleus. This force, called the strong force, is the same one that binds quarks in a proton or neutron. This strong force does not affect electrons or neutrinos. According to Albert Einstein, mass and energy are equivalent ($E=mc^2$).

A particle is "elementary" if there is no further substructure. Knowledge of the neutrino made its entry in 1930, but in 1956 the neutrino was observed or detected by scientists, and over the years its substructure has been defined. (Again, any further discussion is beyond the scope of this discussion.) The important point is that the study of human behavior moves from biology to physics and cannot be completely explained as of this date. I've introduced physics just enough for the reader to see that any explanation will be extremely complicated in the search for truth.

In physics, a theory consists of a precisely and mathematically defined description of how things are. For example, E equals mc squared. Theories are not truth. Newtonian physics fell; Einsteinian physics will, also. The current theory of Darwinian evolution would not be recognizable by Darwin. The mind-brain as a biological computer replaces the spiritual model. Transmitter molecules (atoms) snap into receptors. The morphine molecule, for example, may stimulate a cell involved in producing good feelings and depress one that processes alertness. The brain cell is like the basic chemical "chip" in a computer responding to the flux of neurotransmitters against its surface. Alcoholism is a metabolic disease with genetic foundations. Molecular psychology will be able to answer some problems of criminal behavior. According to an article published by CASAColumbia,[20]

> alcohol and other drugs are significant factors in all crime. In 2006, alcohol and other drugs were involved in these inmate offenses: 78% of violent crimes, 83% of property crimes, 77% of public order, immigration or weapon offenses; and probation/parole violations. ("New CASA," 2010)

Our prisons, if not abolished (as I advocate), should come to resemble mental hospitals. Treatment with antidepressant drugs reduces violence. Doesn't that tell you something?

Read Shengold, *Soul Murder* (1989). What about Richard Odom? Wasn't he a "soul murdered" child? Could an analysis at the molecular level of the amygdala and low serotonin have made a difference between life or death as a penalty? Of course, there may be other experts to testify

---

20 From their website, 2019: "CASAColumbia is a national nonprofit research and policy organization focused on improving the understanding, prevention, and treatment of substance use and addiction. Founded in 1992 by former U.S. Secretary of Health, Education, and Welfare, Joseph A. Califano, Jr., our interdisciplinary experts collaborate with others to promote effective policies and practices. We conduct and synthesize research, inform and guide the public, evaluate and improve health care, and analyze and recommend policies on substance use and addiction. For more information, visit www.centeronaddiction.org."

otherwise, but in the world tomorrow, crime will be explained in detail at the molecular level. (How much longer will it be?) We took the wrong road.

Genes produce the shape, color, and behavior in individuals and in species. In the BBC series *Ascent of Man* (see also the 1973 book by the same name), author Jacob Bronowski says:

> The genes are strung out along the chromosomes, which become visible only when the cell is dividing. But the question is not how the genes are arranged; the modern question is "how do they act?" The genes are made of nucleic acids. That is where the action is....
>
> A young man in his twenties, James Watson, arrives in Cambridge [in the 1950s] and teams up with a man of thirty-five, Francis Crick, to decipher the structure of deoxyribonucleic acid (DNA for short). DNA is a nucleic acid, and it had become clear in the preceding ten years that there, the chemical message is carried from generation to generation....
>
> What is the chemistry and what is the architecture?.... Well, it was clear that DNA is made of sugars and phosphates...and four specific small molecules or bases. Two of them are very small molecules, thymine and cytosine [in each of which atoms of carbon, nitrogen, oxygen, and hydrogen are arranged in a hexagon], and two of them are rather larger, guanine and adenine [in each of which the atoms are arranged as a hexagon and a pentagon joined together]....
>
> But a building is not a heap of stones, and the DNA molecule is not a heap of bases. What gives it its structure and therefore its function? It was clear by then that the DNA molecule is a long, extended chain, but rather rigid, a kind of organic crystal, and

it seemed likely that it would be a helix. How many helixes, how many spirals, in parallel? One? Two? Three? Four?... At the end of 1952, the great genius of structural chemistry, Linus Pauling, in California proposed a three-helix model. The backbone of sugar and phosphate ran down the middle, and the bases stuck out in all directions.

Jim Watson...would go for the double helix; moreover, with the backbones running on the outside—a sort of spiral staircase, with the sugars and phosphates running like two handrails. [There were] agonies of experimentation to see how the bases would fit as the steps in that model. And then all at once it became self-evident. Of course there must be on each step a small base and a large base.... Thymine must be matched by adenine, and if you have cytosine then it must be matched by guanine. The bases go together in pairs of which each determines the other.

So the model of the DNA molecule is a spiral staircase, a right-handed spiral in which each tread is of the same size, at the same distance from the next, and turns at the same rate—thirty-six degrees between treads. And if cytosine is at one end of a tread, then guanine is at the other; and so for the other base pair....

The treads are a code which will tell the cell step-by-step how to make one of the proteins necessary to life.... The handrails of sugars and phosphates hold the spiral staircase rigid on each side. The spiral DNA molecule is a gene, a gene in action, and the treads are the steps by which it acts....

The model patently lends itself to the process of replication, with is fundamental to life.

When a cell divides, the two spirals separate. Each base fixes opposite to it the other member of the pair to which it belongs, so that when a cell divides, the same gene is reproduced. The magic number two...is the means by which a cell passes on its genetic identity when it divides.

[Every cell in the body carries the potential to make the whole animal, except for the sperm and egg cells.] Only the sperm and the egg are incomplete. They are half cells. They carry half the number of genes. Then, when the egg is fertilized by the sperm, the total of DNA instructions is assembled again. The fertilized egg is then a complete cell, and it is the model of every cell in the body. Every cell is formed by division of the fertilized egg, and so it is identical with it in its genetic make-up....

As the embryo develops, the cells differentiate. Along the primitive streak, the beginnings of the nervous system are laid down. Clumps of cells on either side will form the backbone. The cells specialize. Nerve cells. Muscle cells,. Connective tissue, the ligaments and tendons, blood cells, blood vessels. The cells specialize because they have accepted the DNA instructions to make the proteins that are appropriate to the functioning of that cell and no other. This is the DNA in action. The baby is an individual from birth... [and] inherits gifts from both parents....

The DNA spiral...is an instruction, a living mobile to tell the cell how to carry out the processes of life step by step.... The machinery of the cell reads off the treads in order, one after another. A sequence of three acts as a signal to the cell to make one amino acid. As the amino acids are formed in order, they line up and assemble in the cell as proteins. And the proteins are the agents and building blocks of life in the cell. (1975)

XIII

Crime and Ethics

A good defense lawyer is like a mad pit-bull dog
attacking without a conscience.

— Edward Witt Chandler

ETHICS is beyond the scope of this paper. However, I'll briefly comment on the subject. Included in the Appendix of this book [Appendix, pp. 48-53] is my published article "Sex, Death & Lawyers' Ethics." I believe it speaks for itself. There is more to ethics for lawyers than just rules of professional responsibility. I will now try to explain.

One of my favorite books is *The Prince* (1513), written by the Italian Niccolò Machiavelli (1469-1527). The knowledge he achieved was the result of private reading, meditation, and life experiences. His view of politics was largely determined by his own frustrating experience. His career was abruptly ended, and he was deprived of his office and exiled from the city for one year. He then fell under suspicion (unjustly) of being implicated in a conspiracy against a new government. He was arrested, disgraced, imprisoned, tortured on the rack, tried and fined, and then released from a dungeon (thanks to a new Pope). He was later recalled to an active role in public life. In *The Prince* and the *Discourses on Livy* (1517), he expressed his views on a new political morality. He also wrote drama (comedies) and expressed his private amorous adventures in letters.

The Prince established a new science of statesmanship for which the modern world is indebted. To understand the meaning and value of Machiavelli's ideas is beyond the scope of my argument to understand the cause of crime. He wrote many books and articles, but in *The Prince,* he exploits the lesson of history in politics—the morality of politics as opposed to private morality.

According to Machiavelli, politics is an art. One must love the state more than his own soul. Only the prince who has enough military power is able to maintain his dominion. A politician must sometimes caress; sometimes hurt; sometimes forgive; sometimes punish; sometimes benefit; sometimes suppress. Virtue is the essential quality of a prince. A prince should be cruel rather than clement. "It is much safer to be feared than loved," he wrote. A prince should break promises whenever necessary for the welfare of his state.

A prince should imitate the fox and the lion. The fox can protect himself from traps. The lion can defend himself against wolves. Machiavelli gave the world a new science of politics. Politics has a morality of its own.

Now, while *The Prince* is about politics and government (not crime), Machiavelli's ideas can be applied to the prevention and control of crime. For example, his idea that the "end justifies the means" is particularly useful in a discussion of crime and ethics. Does "the end justify the means"? For defense lawyers? For prosecutors? Is there a difference?

Suppose a defense lawyer is representing a client, and the only way to save his life is to cheat? Suppose you are morally against the death penalty. What should you do? Does the "end" "justify the means"? If you break the rules of professional responsibility, you are Robin Hood (robbing the rich for the poor), and if caught, you lose your law license. Is there a choice? What do you do? I'll not try to answer these questions.

I have not done *The Prince* justice. My summary or reference is only intended to shed light on ethical questions involving the criminal defense lawyer. Machiavelli's book is profound. A prosecutor seeks justice. A defense lawyer wants to win. A trial is not a search for truth. The duties are different.

CLARENCE DARROW

This lawyer, born in 1857, is my hero. He died on March 13, 1938, just five days after I was born. No other lawyer in U.S. history has had Darrow's aptitude for history, science, philosophy, and other branches of study. He was also a poet. I'll start with the Scopes Monkey Trial in 1925.

Charles Darwin had proposed a revolutionary way of thinking about life on earth. His theory of evolution was outlined in his famous work of scientific literature, *On the Origin of Species by Means of Natural Selection* (1859). But Darwin's discovery of the guiding principle of evolution and the organization of life contradicted the biblical theory of creation.[21] He had revealed a new design of nature, summarized with the chilling phrase, "survival of the fittest."

Now, jump to Darrow in the 1920s in Tennessee.

THE SCOPES MONKEY TRIAL

In the 1920s, the struggle between creationism and evolution came to a head, largely thanks to the influence of Presbyterian lawyer William Jennings Bryan (1860-1925), a three-time presidential candidate and former secretary of state, who saw evolution as a threat to morality. In 1921, Bryan delivered several anti-evolution lectures in Virginia, as part of a campaign to prevent the teaching of evolution in American universities and schools. His influence on

---

21 The best-known homicide in western civilization is the case of fratricide (Cain killed Abel) as set forth in the Book of Genesis 4:1-6. His punishment was not death but exile. (He went to the land of Nod.) Darrow tried more than 50 capital cases and never lost a one to execution.

university education was limited, but (unfortunately) he had better luck in persuading state governments to introduce laws banning publicly funded schools from teaching evolution.

> That it shall be unlawful for any teacher in any of the
> Universities, Normals and all other public schools
> of the State which are supported in whole or in part
> by the public school funds of the State, to teach any
> theory that denies the Story of the Divine Creation of
> man as taught in the Bible, and to teach instead that
> man has descended from a lower order of animals.
>
> — The Butler Act, enacted by the
64th Tennessee General Assembly
(signed into law on March 21, 1925)

In his book *The Rough Guide to Evolution: Darwin's Big Idea That Changed the World,* Mark Pallen describes one effect of the passing of the Butler Act in 1925:

> The most notorious of these laws, the Butler Act,... made it illegal for publicly funded teachers "to teach any theory that denies the Story of the Divine Creation of man as taught in the Bible, and to teach instead that man has descended from a lower order of animals." During the debate that preceded the vote on the bill, one senator ironically suggested that they should also "prohibit the teaching that the earth is round." The law was challenged a few months later in the famous Scopes Monkey Trial.
>
> The trial arose from a provocative collusion between principles and profit. The American Civil Liberties Union (ACLU) aimed to establish a test case by advertising that they would support anyone who

broke the law. A group of local citizens saw this as a chance to boost the small-town economy of Dayton, Tennessee. They soon recruited local science teacher John Scopes (1900-1970) to their cause and persuaded Scopes that he had already fallen foul of the law by teaching from the state-approved textbook. Scopes was charged and ordered to appear at the county courthouse on July 10. William Jennings Bryan volunteered his services to the prosecution, while the ACLU lawyer Clarence Darrow offered to work *pro bono* for the defense, along with Dudley Malone, an experienced divorce lawyer.

The trial ran for less than a fortnight, but attracted unprecedented media attention with over two hundred reporters and the first-ever radio broadcast of judicial proceedings. Acerbic *Baltimore Sun* reporter H.L. Mencken presented the trial to the public in colourful turns of phrase such as "the infidel Scopes" or "the monkey trial." The prosecution called just four witnesses to establish that Scopes had broken the law. The defense tried to field eight expert witnesses to establish that there was no conflict between evolution and the Bible. However, the prosecution argued— and Judge John Raulston accepted—that such expert opinion was irrelevant to the question of whether Scopes had actually taught about evolution. After Bryan snuck in a jibe that humans were descended "not even from American monkeys, but from old world monkeys," defense lawyer Malone delivered a dramatic speech, seen as the highpoint of the trial, passionately arguing that the Bible belonged to the realm of theology and morality rather than to science.

Towards the end, the trial took a bizarre twist as Darrow questioned Bryan as a witness to the authenticity of the Bible. Sparks flew in the resulting exchange, with Darrow using phrases like "your fool religion" and declaring (presciently, given later history): "We have the purpose of preventing bigots and ignoramuses from controlling the education of the United States." To prevent Bryan from summing up, Darrow waived his right to a closing statement. Instead, Darrow asked the judge to bring the jury in and instruct them to return a guilty verdict, which they did after just nine minutes deliberation. The judge fined Scopes the minimum allowed: just $100.

Bryan died in his sleep a few days after the end of the trial. The following year, the verdict was disallowed on a technicality, so Scopes avoided the $100 fine. (Later Scopes even admitted to being unsure whether he had ever taught evolution!) Nonetheless, the Butler Act, although never again invoked, stayed on the statute books until 1967. And in the aftermath of the trial, states and school districts, particularly in the southern Bible belt, saw to it that the teaching of evolution was excluded from many American public schools for over a quarter of a century. (2009)

The following quotation from the play *Inherit the Wind*, which debuted in 1955 and was based on the Scopes trial, was mentioned in the Foreword of this book, but I will repeat it here. Near the end of the play, the fictional girlfriend of a man who is charged with teaching Darwinism in high school says:

I haven't really thought very much. I was always afraid of what I might think—so it seemed safer not to think at all. But now I know. A thought is like a child inside our body. It has to be born. If it dies inside you, part of you dies, too. Maybe what Mr. Darwin wrote is bad. I don't know. Bad or good, it doesn't make any difference. The ideas have to come out—like children. Some of 'em healthy as a bean plant, some sickly. I think the sickly ideas die mostly, don't you, Bert?

Clarence Darrow, left, and William Jennings Bryan in a Dayton, Tennessee, courtroom during the Scopes trial, 1925.

Associated Press photo.

RESIST NOT EVIL

In 1903, Darrow published a book called *Resist Not Evil*. I obtained a copy in the 1970s. If I have "stolen" any ideas to understand crime, this was the beginning! In *Resist Not Evil*, Darrow concluded Chapter VI, "Remedial Effects of Punishment," as follows:

The tendency to abrogate capital punishment, to improve prisons, to modify sentences, to pardon convicts is all in one direction. It can lead to but one inevitable result, the abolition of all judgment of man by man, the complete destruction of all prisons and the treatment of all men as if each human being was the child of the one loving Father and a part and parcel of the same infinite and mysterious life. (p. 76)

He began Chapter VII, "Cause of Crime," with these observations:

If the punishment of so-called crimes tended in any way to prevent violent acts, this tendency would be manifest in some conclusive way. Whether brother-hood love and non-resistance would lessen crime may be a matter of debate, but that punishment does not lessen it, seems to be as well established as any fact that cannot be absolutely proved. The death penalty was for years drastically enforced for the crime of smuggling, but its enforcement in no way tended to prevent the practice which flourished in spite of executions without number,—the common consciousness would not accept this punishment as just and finally rulers were forced to modify the punishment in self-defense. The punishment of death for larceny did not prevent the crime. Nearly every religion has made its way in the face of the severest penal statutes. Its converts have all been criminals and they have accepted and taught their faith at the risk of life. Every organization of working men has grown up in violation of human laws, and the jails, prisons and scaffolds have been busily engaged in suppressing this species of crime; but in spite of the fact that judges still imprison and execute for this crime, these associations are now almost as firmly established as any institution of the world. All new political ideas, democracy, socialism, nihilism have met the same fate and have made their way regardless of scaffolds and jails. Even in the common crimes, like burglary and larceny, prisons have had no effect. From the dawn of civilization an endless procession of weak and helpless victims, handcuffed, despised and outlawed, have been marching up to prison doors and still the procession comes and goes. Time does not stay nor punishment make it less. In fact the older the community and the better settled and undisturbed its life, the greater the number of these unfortunates whom, for some mysterious reason, the Infinite has decreed a life of shame and a death of ignominy and dishonor. If scaffolds and prisons and judges and jailers have no effect to prevent and lessen crime, common wisdom, to say nothing of humane instincts, ought to seek some other plan. (pp. 77-79)

I'll never forget the first time I read these words. Clarence Darrow is indeed my hero,[22] but my solution to

---

22 According to Arthur Weinberg, in the book *Attorney for the Damned: Clarence Darrow in the Courtroom*,

"Shortly before he died on March 13, 1938, Darrow repeated an oft-made observation on crime and criminals: If doctors were to treat the causes of physical illness as lawyers and judges handle crime, treatment of disease would again be like 'black magic.'

"Federal Judge William H. Holly, friend and former partner... delivered the eulogy at Darrow's funeral, and provided an epitaph which fits the man exactly: 'He loved mercy. We may not know what justice is. No judge who sentences a prisoner to the electric chair is more certain of the righteousness of his judgment than the mob that hangs or burns its victim. Whether the offender is legally executed by the sheriff, or illegally hanged by the mob, we cannot be sure whether it is justice or vengeance that has been satisfied. But mercy is a quality that we can all recognize, and in his heart was infinite pity and mercy for the poor, the oppressed, the weak and erring—all races, all colors, all creeds and all human kind. Clarence Darrow made the way easier for man. He preached not doctrine but love and pity, the only virtues that can make this world any better.'" (p. xxii) crime is different: "Dangerous" humans should be executed not as punishment but because they are dangerous!

> Darrow's writings include:
> *A Persian Pearl: and Other Essays* (1899)
> *Resist Not Evil* (1903)
> *An Eye for an Eye* (1905)
> *Farmington* (1904)
> *Crime, Its Causes and Treatment* (1922)
> *The Story of My Life* (1932)

Kiana Kleganow and Franklin L. Jonas, in their book *People's Lawyers: Crusaders for Justice in American History,* described the one time Darrow was asked to be on the prosecutor's side. In September 1931,

> Thomas H. Massie, a United States Navy lieutenant stationed at Pearl Harbor...and his wife, Thalia Fortescue Massie, attended an informal officers' dance held at the Waikiki Beach Section of Honolulu. Thalia Massie, a twenty-one-year old socialite from Washington, D.C., decided to take a walk before the dance ended. She went only a short distance before she was grabbed by two men, who dragged her to a car. Three other men had remained in the car, and they drove to an isolated area, where she alleged that she was raped. The evidence for rape later turned out to be inconclusive, but she was beaten severely enough to have broken her jaw.
>
> The men left her along the side of a road, and she was able to flag down a car....
>
> The next day, Thalia Massie identified four of the men. On October 12, 1932 [actually it was 1931], they were indicted for rape and assault. The trial began in November, and the case was submitted to a local jury

on December 2. It ended in a mistrial four days later when the jury was unable to reach a verdict. The men were released on bail and instructed to report to court daily until a date had been set for a new trial.

Before the new trial took place, Lieutenant Massie beat up one of the alleged assailants and forced him to confess. But the assailant had pictures taken of the welts and bruises on his back, and the lieutenant's lawyer advised that this "confession" would never stand up in court.

In the meantime, Grace Fortescue, the mother of Thalia Massie, arrived...from Washington, D.C. When she learned about the assault on her daughter,... determined that they be found guilty at the second trial, she persuaded Massie and two American sailors under his command to kidnap Joseph Kahahawii, one of the alleged kidnappers, and force him to confess.

Kahahawii was seized and taken to the house where Grace Fortescue was staying on the island. According to the story told by the defense at the trial, Massie pointed his service revolver at Kahahawii, demanding that he confess. When Kahahawii stated, "Yeah, we done it," the enraged lieutenant killed him with one shot.

While Lieutenant Massie stayed in the house, Grace Fortescue and the two sailors put the body in the trunk of a car and hastened to dispose of it. The car was stopped for speeding, and the body was discovered....

Massie, Fortescue, Jones, and Lord were indicted by a grand jury for second-degree murder. Although Darrow was seventy-five years old and had retired in 1928, he was asked by the defense to represent them....

The trial began in April, and many spectators lined up outside the courthouse to hear Darrow present his case....

Darrow...admitted the guilt of his clients, but pleaded with the jury to understand the mental anguish of Fortescue and Massie. Early in the trial, he called an expert witness who stated that Lieutenant Massie had been brought to a dangerous emotional state by the attack on his wife and his feeling that her attackers would not receive justice....

At the conclusion of the trial, Judge Davis instructed the jury to convict the defendants if they were responsible for the murder, regardless of the provocation. The jury returned a verdict of manslaughter, but recommended leniency.

The defendants served one hour in custody. At the end of the hour, Lawrence M. Judd, the governor of Hawaii, commuted their sentences. The attorney general of the island asked Darrow for help in retrying the alleged assailants...

Darrow declined, pointing out that never in his more than half-century of practice had he ever prosecuted anyone, and it was too late to start now!

DARROW IN HIS OWN DEFENSE

From *Attorney for the Damned: Clarence Darrow in the Courtroom*:

Headline, Chicago Tribune, August 16, 1912:

JURORS WEEP AS DARROW PLEADS

CHICAGO ATTORNEY WINS SYMPATHY
OF MEN IN BOX BELIEVED AGAINST HIM

J.J. McNamara, secretary-treasurer of the International

110

Association of Bridge and Structural Workers (AFL), and his brother, J.B. McNamara, were arrested for dynamiting the Times Building in Los Angeles, creating a blast which killed a score of people.

The violence of feeling which led to the explosion is what Louis Adamic refers to as "dynamite" in labor history—and what Bill Haywood called the "class struggle."

At the time of the explosion, the unions were in a concentrated drive to make Los Angeles a "closed town." The Times, owned by General Harrison Gray Otis, was notoriously anti-union and was the leading exponent of the "open shop" policy in that city.

The American Federation of Labor asked Darrow to defend the brothers.

Darrow came to Los Angeles.

Darrow was charged that year with the crime of jury bribing in Los Angeles, California. He, along with four other attorneys, defended himself. He was found "not guilty."

I don't think Darrow would agree with me in my next chapter, "The Solution to Crime." I believe imprisonment for life is worse than death by execution. Would Darrow agree? Would he agree that killing "dangerous" criminals was acceptable? Remember, Darrow knew nothing about DNA, epigenetics, or anything that we have learned in the last 80 years.

When the first U.S. Congress met in 1789, there were only three federal crimes: treason, counterfeiting currency, and smuggling to avoid tariffs. Today, Congress passes more than 2,500 statues each year, and the bureaucracies Congress has spawned churn out more than 65,000 pages of regulations that carry the force of law. Many of these statutes and regulations impose criminal sanctions for their violation.

According to an article on the Smithsonian website,

"American Incarceration," in 2016, 2.7 million American children had a parent behind bars, and 2.2 million humans were in prisons and jails. (China had 1.5 million.) The incarceration rate in the U.S. was 690 out of every 100,000 humans while Russia had a rate of 440. This rate has increased six times over the past century! The U.S. has the world's highest incarceration rate for women!

It took nearly 900 years for the population of the world to reach 1 billion. It took a century and a half to climb to more than six times that. In 1000, the population of the world was estimated to be 300 million. In 1806, the population reached 1 billion. In 2000, the U.N. projection for the world's population was 6.06 billion, and in 2019 the Worldometer website says that there are 7.7 billion people on the planet. Would Darrow be astonished by these numbers?

BAD SEED DEFENSE: LEOPOLD AND LOEB

In one of Darrow's other famous cases (1924), he used in mitigation of punishment the claim of "bad seed" for two boys in Chicago that had pled "guilty," and the only question was punishment—life or death. Of course, he knew nothing about DNA, genetics, or epigenetics, but he successfully argued before the Judge that they each had a "bad seed," resulting in life for each as opposed to death. They had kidnapped and murdered a younger boy to see how it felt. This, of course, stimulated my thinking years ago.

A pair of glasses linked Nathan Leopold, Jr. (age 18) to the crime. He was the son of a Chicago millionaire. Richard Loeb (age 17), son of a vice-president of Sears, Roebuck, and Co., was linked to the crime by Leopold, and both boys soon "confessed" to the kidnapping and murder of Bobby Franks (age 14), son of a prominent and respected Chicago businessman. The maximum penalty in Illinois was death by hanging. Would it be life or death?

Richard Loeb had wanted to commit the "perfect crime": kidnapping, murder, ransom. Nathan Leopold, Jr. agreed to help. They had, by telephone, attempted to obtain $10,000 ransom from Bobby Frank's father, but the dead body was discovered before the pay-off. The crime was committed for the "sake of a thrill," they said afterward.

Both teenagers were brilliant students. Leopold was the youngest graduate of the University of Chicago. Loeb was the youngest to graduate from the University of Michigan. Darrow (age 67) agreed to defend the boys.

The trial began July 21, 1924, in Cook County, Illinois. The defendants both pled "guilty." From *Attorney for the Damned* (p. 19):

Darrow began his summation August 22, 1924. The afternoon newspaper carried a banner head:

```
DARROW PLEADS FOR MERCY: MOBS RIOT
```

It then went on in a sub-headline:

```
BAILIFF'S ARM BROKEN AND WOMAN FAINTS
  AS FRENZIED MOB STORMS PAST GUARDS;
     JUDGE CALLS FOR 20 POLICE;
      FEARS SOME WILL BE KILLED
```

More people than all the courtrooms in the old Cook County Court building could accommodate mobbed Judge Caverly's court when it was learned Darrow was to speak.

The crowd "fought like animals to…hear Darrow speak," a newspaper reported.

Judge Caverly himself found it hard to get into the courtroom. So did Nathan Leopold, Sr. and his son Foreman. Assistant State's Attorney Savage had to fight his way in.

Judge Caverly ordered the courtroom doors closed. The bailiff protested: "Judge, there are four of your friends outside."

"Let them stay outside," snapped Judge Caverly.

As the veteran attorney pleaded for the boys' lives, Loeb dug his fist in his eyes, and Leopold unsuccessfully tried to hold back tears.

Judge Caverly sat on the bench, chin cupped in his right hand. Attentive. Watching.

From the same book, in the words of Clarence Darrow:

"You may stand them up on the trap door of the scaffold, and choke them to death, but that act will be infinitely more cold-blooded, whether justified or not, than any act that these boys have committed or can commit....

"Talk about scheming. Yes, it is the scheme of disease; it is the scheme of infancy; it is the scheme of fools; it is the scheme of irresponsibility from the time it was conceived until the last act of the tragedy....

"But we are told that they planned. Well, what does that mean? A maniac plans, an idiot plans, an animal plans, any brain that functions may plan; but their plans were the diseased plans of the diseased mind....

"You can trace it all down through the history of man. You can trace the burnings, the boilings, the drawings and quarterings, the hanging of people in England at the crossroads, carving them up and hanging them as examples for all to see.

"We can come down to the last century when nearly two hundred crimes were punishable by death, and by death in every form; not only hanging—that was too humane—but burning, boiling, cutting into pieces, torturing in all conceivable forms.

"You can read the stories of the hangings on a high hill, and the populace for miles around coming out to the scene, that everybody might be awed into goodness. Hanging for picking pockets—and more pockets were picked in the crowd that went to the hanging than had been known before. Hangings for murder—and men were murdered on the way there and on the way home. Hanging for poaching, hanging for everything, and hangings in public, not shut up cruelly and brutally in a jail, out of the light of day, wakened in the nighttime and led forth and killed, but taken to the shire town on a high hill, in the presence of a multitude, so that all might see that the wages of sin were death....

"The child is gradually taught, and habits are built up. These habits are supposed to be strong enough so that they will form inhibitions against conduct when the emotions come in conflict with the duties of life. Dr. Singer and Dr. Church, both of them, admitted exactly what I am saying now. The child of himself knows nothing about right and wrong, and the teaching built up gives him habits, so he will be able to control certain instincts that surge upon him, and which surge upon everyone who lives. If the instinct is strong enough and the habit weak enough, the habit goes down before it. Both of these eminent men admit it. There can be no question about it. His conduct depends upon the relative strength of the instinct and the habit that has been built up....

"On Sunday, June first, before any of the friends of these boys or their counsel could see them, while they were in the care of the state's attorney's office, they brought them in to be examined by these alienists. I am not going to discuss that in detail as I may later on. Dr. Patrick said that the only unnatural he noted about it was that they had no emotional reactions. Dr. Church

115

said the same. These are their alienists, not ours. These boys could tell this gruesome story without a change of countenance, without the slightest feelings. There were no emotional reactions to it. What was the reason? I do not know. How can I tell why? I know what causes the emotional life. I know it comes from the nerves, the muscles, the endocrine glands, the vegetative system. I know it is the most important part of life. I know it is practically left out of some. I know that without it men cannot live. I know that without it they cannot act with the rest. I know they cannot feel what you feel and what I feel; that they cannot feel the moral shocks which come to men who are educated and who have not been deprived of an emotional system or emotional feelings.... Is Dickie Loeb to blame because out of the infinite forces that conspired to form him, the infinite forces that were at work producing him ages before he was born, that because out of these infinite combinations he was born without it? If he is, then there should be a new definition for justice. Is he to blame for what he did not have and never had? Is he to blame that his machine is imperfect? Who is to blame? I do not know. I have never in my life been interested so much in fixing blame as I have in relieving people from blame. I am not wise enough to fix it....It may be defective nerves. It may be a defective heart or liver. It may be defective endocrine glands. I know it is something. I know that nothing happens in this world without a cause.

"I know, Your Honor, that if you, sitting here in this court, and in this case, had infinite knowledge, you could lay your fingers on it, and I know you would not visit it on Dickie Loeb. I asked Dr. Church and I asked Dr. Singer whether, if they were wise enough to know, they could not find the cause, and both of them said yes.

I know that they and Loeb are just as they are, and that they did not make themselves. There are at least two theories of man's responsibility. There may be more. There is the old theory that if a man does something it is because he willfully, purposely, maliciously, and with a malignant heart sees fit to do it. And that goes back to the possession of man by devils. The old indictments used to read that a man being possessed of a devil did so and so. But why was he possessed with the devil? Did he invite him in? Could he help it?

"Very few half-civilized people believe that doctrine any more. Science has been at work, humanity has been at work, scholarship has been at work, and intelligent people now know that every human being is the product of the endless heredity back of him and the infinite environment around him. He is made as he is and he is the sport of all that goes before him and is applied to him, and under the same stress and storm you would act one way and I act another, and poor Dickie Loeb another...

"These boys—I do not care what their mentality; that simply makes it worse—are emotionally defective. Every single alienist who has testified in this case has said so. The only person who did was not Dr. Krohn. While I am on that subject, lest I forget the eminent doctor, I want to refer to one or two things. In the first place, all these alienists that the State called came into the state's attorney's office and heard these boys tell their story of this crime, and that is all they heard....

"To believe that any boy is responsible for himself or his early training is an absurdity that no lawyer or judge should be guilty of today. Somewhere this came to the boy. If his failing came from his heredity, I do not know where or how. None of us are bred perfect and pure; and the color of our hair, the color of our eyes, our stature, the weight and fineness of our brain, and everything about us could, with full knowledge, be traced with absolute certainty to somewhere. If we had the pedigree it could be traced just the same in a boy as it could in a dog, a horse or a cow.

"I do not know what remote ancestors may have sent down the seed that corrupted him, and I do not know through how many ancestors it may have passed until it reached Dickie Loeb.

"All I know is that it is true, and there is not a biologist in the world who will not say that I am right."

DARROW'S ARGUMENT

Darrow in an extremely passionate speech argued against the death penalty. He mentioned that Leopold was planning to start Harvard Law School. He admitted they had murdered a little boy against whom they had nothing. He argued that the boys were mentally diseased. (Apparently, he had expert testimony from psychiatrists.) He argued that the boys "did not reason" and that "they could not reason." There was no way to justify the murder.

Darrow said they killed the little boy as "they might kill a spider or a fly, for the experience." He mentioned the names of his expert witnesses, Dr. White, Dr. Glueck, and Dr. Healy, and their opinion that the accused boys were "driven by some force." He said there were only two theories: "their diseased brains drove them to it" or "possession by devils."

Bobby Franks went to school and never came back to his home. They hunted someone to kill—for nothing. Darrow did not assert the insanity defense. He did describe the killing "as a mad act of a child." There was no motive or reason. There was no question of revenge or any motive or reason. He compared the killing to the "mad acting of the fool in King Lear." Darrow argued you need no experts, no x-rays, "no study of the endocrines"—their conduct showed exactly what happened. Their plans were the plans of a "diseased mind." They left the body in a culvert. They took the life of Bobby Franks for nothing.

On September 10, 1924, the judge sentenced the defendants to imprisonment for life on the murder charge and 99 years on the kidnapping charge. They were taken to Joliet penitentiary (Illinois). Twelve years later, Loeb was killed in a prison fight. Leopold was eventually released from prison.

My analysis of Darrow's argument does not do it justice. He argued that these boys were born of a "bad seed." Today experts can explain much better the operation of the brain and its defects.

WHAT DARROW AND CHARLES DARWIN DID NOT KNOW

In his "bad seed" theory, Darrow lacked the knowledge of modern man: 46 chromosomes, 20,000 genes, 3.2 billion pairs of chemicals called DNA! DNA was in its infancy (if at all known). Charles Darwin would be surprised with such knowledge. Interestingly, studies of the DNA molecule have supported the theory of Darwinian evolution. We evolved. We are animals. We are mammals. So say the scientific studies of DNA. Studies of our genes have supported my theory of the cause of crime.

Thomas Jefferson said it would take 2,000 years to settle the West. Wouldn't he be surprised! No one knows what tomorrow will bring. What will the next human species be like—after replacing *Homo sapiens*? It's billions of years before our sun dies and with it Earth. In the meantime, will we be "awakened" and adopt a new method in the war against crime? The control and prevention of crime demands a new strategy. Why wait?

Darrow did not know about the double helix of DNA and that unwound it would stretch to the sun and back 400 times! He did not know that there were 20,000 genes (DNA) in each cell, each gene producing one or more proteins. He did not know how DNA worked. He did not even know the capacity of the brain. We now have a much better understanding of the brain.

OTHER ETHICAL ISSUES

There are other ethical issues involving genetic engineering, and there are those who would even consider the transplanting of heads![23] In the future, society will face many different issues if the control and prevention of crime is as I envision.

A detailed analysis of these ethical issues is beyond the scope of my understanding the cause of crime.

---

23 Transplanting a head might not be enough. For example: Hormones are chemical messengers produced by the endocrine system that regulate various functions throughout the body. The release of hormones is governed by a very sensitive feedback system, which is controlled by the hypothalamus and pituitary gland in the brain. When hormones are produced in excess or in too limited supply, certain body functions won't work as well as they should. Depression is one of the potential side effects of a hormonal imbalance. The butterfly-shaped thyroid gland in the neck produces hormones that regulate growth, metabolism, and mood. When this gland is underactive (hypothyroidism) or overactive (hyperthyroidism), one of the symptoms may be depression. Disorders of the parathyroid glands (hyperparathyroidism) and adrenal glands (Cushing's disease) also can lead to depression. What else in the body as opposed to the brain is involved in decision-making?

XIV

The Solution to Crime

Biology is to crime as physics is to baseball.

— Unknown author

MOST SCIENTISTS OR EXPERTS believe that the cause of human behavior is fifty percent genetics (and epigenetic?) and fifty percent life experiences or environment. I believe that genetics (and epigenetics), or what we inherit, is ninety percent, and life experiences (environment) is only ten percent. Either way, "free will" is a myth, and crime is not the individual's "fault." We need to control and prevent crime by a different approach. This is my solution.

Ninety percent of all crimes committed go undetected. Of the ten percent detected, ninety-nine percent plea "guilty" and get a bargain—a better sentence or probation. (Why?) The remaining one percent go to trial and are found guilty by His Honor or in the case of most serious crimes a jury, twelve members of the community. But we can't read minds, and even with 3,000 or so rules of evidence, it's hard to reach the truth. The rules of evidence and procedure ought to be abandoned and rewritten. Most citizens do not even realize what's happening. Fair trials just don't exist, because of ignorance, bias, and dishonesty. How do I know this? It is simply my opinion, based on 40 years of experience as a criminal defense lawyer and college teacher of criminal justice. I've also done a lot of critical thinking on my own, late at night, when I couldn't sleep.

We have lost the war against crime. Statistics clearly show this result. Society went down the wrong road. We need to rethink our approach and focus on the biological cause(s) of crime with the intent to help people, not punish them. God will punish all sinners (criminals) in the end, unless by grace they are saved. No one just escapes, but punishment has not stopped criminal behavior. Criminals are not just "morally weak" sinners.

What do we do? Destroy ninety percent or more of our prisons. Modernize jails. (Remember that the accused are presumed innocent.) At trial, three judges would act like medical doctors, psychiatrists, or psychologists, with the goal to rehabilitate and "save" the guilty. Scientists and other experts would testify. Each judge would retire to a separate room to write his/her opinion. They would then meet to discuss a verdict. These judges can find the accused "not guilty" or "guilty." If "guilty," the individual goes home with an electronic bracelet (GPS) for the rest of his life, or is executed in the next room with a 13 cent bullet in the back of his head! The issue would be how dangerous the person is to others.

No more trial by jury or just an untrained judge. Ignorance, bias, and dishonesty are gone. These judges would be trained and educated to be fair and honest. A university degree (four to six years) would be required, with special education like doctors and lawyers today.

We don't need prisons. No more executions just to "punish." Billions and billions saved would go back to the schools and communities to prevent crime by education. Mothers, fathers, and children would go to school to learn how to live without criminal behavior. Juvenile delinquents would get the most attention. They would be treated as adults with juvenile brains. No more lawyers. They are gone. Instead, neuroscientists, social workers, investigators, and all the technology available would take their place.

What I also would like to see is a one-hour class covering the definition of crimes and human behavior each week, each year, from the age of six until the person graduates from high school. This is a beginning. Most criminals are juvenile delinquents before they begin a life of crime, be it murder, burglary, rape, or DUI. It is complicated. It is difficult. One of the first problems is how to define "dangerous." A dictionary will not help. The definitions of words vary. For example, "abuse of power" is defined differently than "child abuse." "Domestic abuse" is when one partner controls the other. Mere conflict is not abuse. "Traumatic Brain Injury" (TBI) is described as blunt or blast force applied to the head, transmitting force to the brain, causing injury. "Tinnitus" is an auditory perception in the absence of any external sound stimulus. Tinnitus can be also be defined as a phantom perception of sound. Can "dangerous" be defined in such simple terms? Or is it impossible? (I'll not try.)

So, how do you define "dangerous"? And this might vary from state to state. Another problem: Who decides who is to live or die—who is "dangerous"? Three judges?

Science is evolving. Biologists would study living cells to diagnose and treat criminal behavior. Scientists in universities and start-up companies would lead the way. Biologists would go well beyond genetic engineering that just "knocks out" a bad gene or inserts another. Society will solve the problems of over-population, and babies that are "defective" will not even be born. If cancer, inflammatory diseases, and rare metabolic disorders can be identified, so can criminal tendencies. It's biology. Biology is to crime as physics is to baseball. The answer is in deoxyribonucleic acid—DNA!

Every cell in your body is a little computer. The gene (DNA) is expressed by being transcribed into RNA and then translated into protein molecules. Out comes a squirt of hormone from a gland cell, an electrical impulse from a nerve cell, a stream of antibodies from an immune cell, and so on.

In 1953, molecular biologists James Watson and Francis Crick published a discovery that was critical to our scientific understanding of life. Building on the work of other DNA researchers,[24] they described the double-helical structure of DNA, which is found in the nucleus of cells and mitochondria. Cells are in a sense "libraries" that contain encoded information. A new era in biology began.

How much information does DNA hold? According to Bernd-Olaf Küppers, in his book *Information and the Origins of Life*, "the molecular text describing the construction of a bacterial cell would be about the size of a thousand-page book." How does the genome of a human compare? "In the human genome, there are more than a thousand million molecular symbols encoding the hereditary information. This would fill a library of several thousand volumes." To describe the writing in DNA as "molecular-genetic language" is more than mere metaphor. Küppers continues: "Like human language, the molecular-genetic language also possesses a syntactic dimension."

Another source has explained how this works in a fairly simple manner:

> Information, whether in the form of pictures, sounds, or words, can be stored and processed in many ways. Computers, for example, do this all digitally. Living cells store and process information chemically, DNA being the key compound.

---

24 In 1869, chemist Johann Friedrich Miescher identified what we now call DNA. In 1881, Albrecht Kossel identified nuclein as a nucleic acid and provided its present chemical name, DNA. He also isolated the five nucleotides adenine, cytosine, guanine, thymine, and uracil (A, C, G, T, and U). In the early 1900s, biochemist Phoebus Levene discovered the order of certain chemical components of DNA and how these combine to form a chain-like molecule. In 1950, biochemist Erwin Chargaff discovered that the composition of DNA varies among species, and in 1951, Rosalind Franklin's x-ray image of DNA enabled James Watson, Francis Crick, and Maurice Wilkins to deduce the structure of DNA. (Information gleaned from several sources, including (Lee, 2013)

How do cells use information? Think of DNA as a collection of recipes, each one involving step-by-step processes, with each step carefully scripted in precise terms. But instead of the end result being a cake or a cookie, it might be a cabbage or a cow. In living cells, of course, the processes are fully automated, adding yet another layer of complexity and sophistication....

Put simply, DNA has a "grammar," or set of rules, that strictly regulates how its instructions are composed and carried out.

The "words" and "sentences" in DNA make up the various "recipes" that direct the production of proteins and other substances that form the building blocks of the various cells that make up the body. For example, the "recipe" might guide the production of bone cells, muscle cells, nerve cells, or skin cells. "The filament of DNA is information, a message written in a code of chemicals, one chemical for each letter," wrote evolutionist Matt Ridley. "It is almost too good to be true, but the code turns out to be written in a way that we can understand." ("Your cells," 2019)

The use of biocomputing has yet to even be conceived. We have only begun to understand the biology of human behavior, including criminal behavior. We are deeply indebted to Charles Darwin and his research, as well as countless others at such institutions as MIT, Harvard, Princeton, and the University of California, Berkley, who work daily to solve human problems. But society is 200 or more years away from genetic engineering as a solution to crime. It will happen, but between now and then what do we do to solve the problem? (We could begin by studying quantum physics to understand consciousness.)

There will be no right to remain silent. This is one of many constitutional rights that will be abolished. Lawyers will become dinosaurs and evolve into scientists who would aid the court (the judges) in rendering a decision. Policemen would be more like emergency medical technicians, with more formal education and training, who understand that the human decision-making process is biological. Many rules of procedures would have to be rewritten. Different states could try different approaches so we could see what works best. Due process would be gone, and the Bill of Rights of the Constitution would be abolished. The goal? Make it a better world—a better USA!

But we need to take our heads out of the sand and think. Critically think. In the solution to crime, truth is easy to define. Justice isn't; nor mercy. Justice is possible. Remember: Biology is to crime as physics is to baseball. It's a matter of understanding how crime works. The goal, to control and prevent crime—not punish. Punishment is God's business.

> *The thing in life is to find what is really important and to disregard the rest.*
>
> — Unknown

> *Most of the important things that a human being ought to know cannot be comprehended by youth.*
>
> — Robert Hutchins, President, University of Chicago

XV

Conclusion

The long habit of doing something wrong gives it the superficial appearance of being right.

— Thomas Paine[25]

IN 1992, Pope John Paul II closed a 13-year investigation into the Church's 1633 condemnation of Galileo, an Italian scientist. Galileo was forgiven for advocating that the Earth revolved around the sun.

In 1610, Galileo had published and declared that the moon had mountains and valleys like the Earth. He also said that four satellites revolved around Jupiter. In 1613, he published his observations that Venus has phases like our moon. This could only happen if both Venus and Earth revolved around the sun.

Church doctrine at the time was that the Earth was

---

25 Thomas Paine (1737-1809), born in England, played an important role in both the American and French Revolutions. He was among the most influential authors and reformers of his age. In 1774, he emigrated to America where he helped edit the *Pennsylvania Magazine*. From the back cover of the Dover Edition of *Common Sense*: "On January 10, 1776, he published his pamphlet *Common Sense*, a persuasive argument for the colonies' political and economic separation from Britain. *Common Sense* critics the evils of monarchy, accuses the British government of inflicting economic and social injustices upon the colonies, and points to the absurdity of an island attempting to rule a continent. Credited by George Washington as having changed the minds of many of his countrymen, the document sold over 500,000 copies with a few months." *Common Sense* remains a landmark document in the struggle for freedom. Even so, his view on religion caused many of his friends to abandon him in his later years. It is reported that only six people showed up to his funeral, half of them former slaves.

the center of all motion, and in 1616, the Church issued a warning to Galileo. In 1633, the Inquisition condemned him to house arrest for life. He was exonerated more than 350 years later for the Church's mistake!

Galileo was placed under house arrest for supporting the Copernican model of our solar system. Such punishment was a mistake. It is also a mistake to punish criminals rather than treat them as if they suffered from illness. Whether you believe in God the Creator[26] or that evolution just happened does not matter.

What is important is to recognize that as humans we also went down the wrong road in the war against crime, adopting punishment as a means to protect mankind from mankind. We are animals. We are mammals. We evolved.[27] Crime is in our DNA.

Scientists observe and use the scientific method to

---

26 At some point in time, Jesus came to be considered God. The divinity of Jesus was first conceived by his followers. This conception was refined to become the core of Christian theology and the core of our culture, our thought, our world. The New Testament, a collection of 27 books written in Koine Greek between A.D. 60 and A.D. 150, is one of the most important and influential works in all of history. Was it a book of faith or a cultural artifact? The New Testament is one of the least clearly understood books in history. It is widely disputed.

27 Darwinian evolution is the theory that species evolve by natural selection, named after the English naturalist Charles Robert Darwin, who expounded the theory in 1859 in his book *The Origin of Species by Means of Natural Selection or the Preservation of Favored Races in this Struggle for Life*. Survival of the fittest is an informal description of natural selection, referring to the fact that the fittest organisms in the struggle for existence live longest and therefore transmit more of their genetic characteristics to future generations. The phrase was coined not by Darwin but by the English philosopher Herbert Spencer (1820-1903) in his *Principles of Biology* (1864). In the 6th and final edition of *Origin of Species*, Darwin changed the title of his Chapter 4 from "Natural Selection" to "Natural Selection and the Survival of the Fittest."

establish theories and laws. You must understand evolution to understand yourself. There are 100 million galaxies in our universe. (There are many universes.) There are, alone, 100 billion suns in our galaxy, the "Milky Way"! In our sun, there are trillions of hydrogen atoms being converted into helium atoms. The surface of the sun is very hot, but the core of Earth is hotter! Our universe is 15 billion years old. Our sun is 6 billion years old. Earth is 4 billion, and life on Earth is 3.8 billion. Humans have been around 7 million years. They were each made of trillions of invisible cells and were covered with trillions of microscopic single-cell creatures and evolved from an ape.

We originated in Africa. We spread all over the world without cars or trucks. We walked or ran or moved by boat. We belonged to a group of animals, primates. We know this from genetics (DNA) and fossils, bones. In fact, 4-7 million years ago, we shared a common ancestor with chimpanzees. (We are indeed a third chimpanzee.) Our primate cousins included chimps, gorillas, and orangutans. We indeed were apes! We evolved. To understand, you must read Darwin's *Origin of Species* and learn the theory of natural selection. We are at the top of the food chain. With technology, we have advanced beyond belief. Remember the vacuum tube of the 1950s? In those days, no one (including myself) could even imagine what would happen—micro-electronics, mobile phones, cell towers, etc.

Biology is to crime as physics is to baseball. According to David Eagleman, in his quotation at the beginning of the book *The Power and Grace Between Nasty or Nice* by John C. Friel, Ph.D. and Linda D. Olund Friel, M.A.,

> If you are a carrier of a particular set of genes, the probability that you will commit a violent crime is four times as high as it would be if you lacked those genes. You're three times as likely to commit aggravated

assault, eight times as likely to be arrested for murder, and 13 times as likely to be arrested for a sexual offense. The overwhelming majority of prisoners carry these genes; 98.1 percent of death-row inmates do.

We need to abolish the senseless search for "justice" and solve the crime problem with logic, reason, and common sense. Science, not religion, is the solution to a better world—less crime. Criminal responsibility should not be based on the "free will" God gave to man, despite Blackstone's *Commentaries on the Laws of England* (1765-69).[28] Man does not have "free will," nor do any of our animal kin. He has DNA. In 50 to 200 years, we will understand the relationship of the conscious brain to the unconscious brain, and perhaps the human decision-making process, and take one or several giant leaps and really understand crime. Its secret is in DNA.

Early in my life as a criminal defense lawyer, I decided that some criminals had a genetic defect as a cause of their crime(s). Recently I concluded that I was wrong and also that all humans are born criminals and only some have biological defects. We are animals. We are mammals. We evolved. Today we have the brain of the caveman—all of us! What's the difference then, if any, among individuals? We do not have free will. Some of us behave, and some of us do not. Why?

I don't know. It will be 50 to 200 years before that question can be answered. In the meantime, defense lawyers must consider the role of biology in the cause of crime as best as we can. Society is not yet ready to change how it prevents and controls crime. We must work as best we can within

---

28 Sir William Blackstone (1723-1780) was an influential British jurist and a legal professor at Oxford. His *Commentaries* are among the first historical accounts of English law and the first systemization analysis of the English legal system. We adopted that system.

the idea of punishment for criminals until society sees the light. Hopefully, scientists and experts will discover how the conscious (1/8) brain communicates with the unconscious (7/8) brain, and how the decision-making process works. For some, we can then cure the biological cause of their criminal behavior by genetic engineering, or if necessary and feasible, transplanting their head! For others, it's execution, because they are as dangerous as a rattlesnake. The questions will be: How do we decide who is dangerous? What's the definition of dangerous? I actually believe this will happen.

Our species will be replaced. We eventually will become extinct (if not destroyed) when the Earth is destroyed as the sun dies, millions or billions of years from now. The planets as they move in their orbits lose energy, so that year by year their orbits get smaller and smaller, and they eventually will fall into the sun (if it's still there). How long before we wake up and realize we went down the wrong road to prevent and control crime?

Read *The Brain Defense* (2017) by Kevin Davis, a Chicago-based journalist and the author of *Defending the Damned* and *The Wrong Man*. His award-winning writing has appeared in *USA Today*, the *Chicago Tribune*, the *Utne Reader*, *Chicago Magazine*, *The Rumpus*, *Writer's Digest*, and other publications. He is a former staff reporter for the *Sun-Sentinel* in South Florida and is an editor at the *ABA Journal*. I obtained a copy of *The Brain Defense* from my good friend Marvin Massey, as a gift after I had written a draft of *Understanding Crime*. Wow! This book is extremely well-written and is explosive as to the cause of crime, though his view is different than mine.

From Kevin Davis's website:

In 1991, the police were called to East 72nd St. in Manhattan, where a woman's body had fallen from a twelfth-story window. The woman's husband, Herbert Weinstein, soon confessed to having hit and strangled his wife after an argument, then dropping her body out of their apartment window to make it look like a suicide. The 65-year-old Weinstein, a quiet, unassuming retired advertising executive, had no criminal record, no history of violent behavior—not even a short temper. How, then, to explain this horrific act?

Journalist Kevin Davis uses the perplexing story of the Weinstein murder to present a riveting, deeply researched exploration of the intersection of neuroscience and criminal justice. Shortly after Weinstein was arrested, an MRI revealed a cyst the size of an orange on his brain's frontal lobe, the part of the brain that governs judgment and impulse control. Weinstein's lawyer seized on that discovery, arguing that the cyst had impaired Weinstein's judgment and that he should not be held criminally responsible for the murder....

The Weinstein case marked the dawn of a new era in America's courtrooms, raising complex and often troubling questions about how we define responsibility and free will, how we view the purpose of punishment, and how strongly we are willing to bring scientific evidence to bear on moral questions.

Davis brings to light not only the intricacies of the Weinstein case but also the broader history linking brain injuries and aberrant behavior, from the bizarre stories of Phineas Gage and Charles Whitman, perpetrator of the 1966 Texas Tower Sniper Massacre, to the role that brain damage may play in violence carried out by football players and troubled veterans of America's twenty-first century wars....

Criminal lawyers are increasingly turning to neuroscience and new technologies like MRIs to introduce the effects of brain injuries into the courtroom. Some are caused by trauma or by tumors, cancer, or drug or alcohol abuse, with new diagnoses like CTE and TBI, as well as PTSD. Lawyers argue that brain damage should be considered in determining guilt or innocence, the death penalty or years behind bars. As he takes stock of the past, present and future of neuroscience in the courts, Davis offers a powerful account of its potential and its hazards.

Thought-provoking and brilliantly crafted, *The Brain Defense* marries a true crime murder mystery complete with colorful characters and courtroom drama with a sophisticated discussion of how our legal system has changed—and must continue to change— as we broaden our understanding of the human mind.

Also, remember Adrian Raine's *The Anatomy of Violence,* and read "Searching for the Mark of Cain" [Appendix, p. 37] by Martin Enserink, *Science* (pp. 575-577), July 28, 2000. I am not the "lone ranger."

> *Every sentence that I utter should be regarded by you not as an assertion but as a question.*
>
> — Niels Bohr

I, Edward Witt Chandler, am not a scientist. I am not an expert. What I have said is based upon what I have read and my 40 years of experience as a lawyer.

What causes crime? Most of us believe the Titanic sank in 1912 because it hit an iceberg. No, it didn't sink because it hit an iceberg. It sank because the humans who built the ship made the metal hull with thinner metal than designed and required by the architects. (Why? So the ship would cross the Atlantic faster.) The cause of the sinking was human error. If built according to the specifications of its designer, according to men of science today, it would have survived the collision with the iceberg. The actual cause: human error. So, what is the actual cause of crime? Start with the "iceberg." The human brain is 1/8 conscious and 7/8 unconscious, like the iceberg. (You can only see 1/8 of the iceberg. The rest is submerged.) So, the cause of a crime? We will never know until we know the relationship between the conscious brain and the unconscious brain. Fifty years? One hundred years? Who knows? But I can speculate or hypothesize: It will happen before the sun burns out!

In conclusion, I quote Albert Einstein, from his letter to a grieving father, February 12, 1950, as most accurately translated in Alice Calaprice's (2005) book, *The New Quotable Einstein*:

A human being is part of the whole, called by us "Universe", a part limited in time and space. He experiences himself, his thoughts and feelings as something separate from the rest—a kind of optical delusion of his consciousness. The striving to free oneself from this delusion is the one issue of true religion. Not to nourish it but to try to overcome it is the way to reach the attainable measure of peace of mind. (p. 206)

Acknowledgments

Writing is like driving at night in the fog. You can only see as far as your headlights, but you can make the whole trip that way.

— E.L. Doctorow

BOOKS that I have recently acquired that opened my mind include Niehoff, *The Biology of Violence* (1999); Raine, *The Anatomy of Violence* (2013); Davis, *The Brain Defense* (2017); and Sapolsky, *Behave* (2007). My view is different from theirs. It is based upon my experience of 40 years as a criminal defense lawyer and my education, as well as the ideas of others. I know this, despite no scientific experiments or empirical data to back up some of my conclusions and opinions. I'm not a scientist or expert. If I have erred, those errors can be sorted out by others. It's like Isaac Newton discovering "gravitation." The apple fell from the tree, like all falling objects, perpendicular to the earth. It would be years before his hypothesis was established theory, and there are those who still disagree.

President Harry S. Truman's best expert on "explosions" said that the atomic bombs would not explode, but later they did over Japan in 1945. Einstein made 23 or more "mistakes," but his theories revolutionized science (e.g., he divided one by zero, which cannot be done). I'm a grain of sand compared to these intellectual giants, but I believe in my idea as to the cause of crime. What's important is not that you agree or disagree, whether I'm right or wrong, but that we are thinking critically. Questions are more important than answers.

Credit must also be given to continuing legal education programs I have attended and the lawyers I have been privileged to teach with and learn from, as well as many books and articles. For that reason, it must be said that there are now probably very few original ideas, and the ideas I have expressed here are largely influenced by what I have learned from others—except the idea for this paper is "original."

In 1977-1978, I became aware of a discipline called sociobiology. I purchased the 1975 book on the subject, *Sociobiology: The New Synthesis* by Edward O. Wilson (University Research Professor Emeritus at Harvard); also, later, a 1979 book by David Barash, *The Whisperings Within: Evolution and the Origin of Human Nature*. My mind nearly exploded. Dr. Barash was a professor of psychology and zoology at the University of Washington, his Ph.D. in zoology was from the University of Washington, and he had published another book, *Sociology and Behavior*.

Barash's book *The Whisperings Within* begins by quoting Albert Einstein, Pope Pius XII, and the wife of the Bishop of Worchester. The book is a powerful look or speculative excursion into human sociobiology. It was an invitation to explore the latest findings (as of 1979) of genetics and ecology as applied to human behavior. ("Sociobiology" is defined as the application of evolutionary principles to social behavior including the human animal.)

The book was fascinating. I had just graduated from the University of Washington with a graduate law degree (LL.M.) in law and marine affairs. My mind was wide open. His stories of rape in ducks, adultery in bluebirds, prostitution in hummingbirds, divorce and lesbian pairing in gulls, homosexual rape in parasitic worms, why gorillas have small testicles while those of chimpanzees are enormous, and how male coral fish pretend to be fierce to impress the females was intended to help the reader to "know yourself better." I was amazed to find how applicable his book was to my interest in human behavior as a criminal defense lawyer.

It was a wake-up call. My new degree in law and marine affairs had taken me in a different direction, but I ended up back in Tennessee as a criminal defense lawyer for 40 years, for personal reasons. My approach to the cause of crime was biological. His discussion of "physics envy" (many of the sciences were not as firmly grounded in physics) is still valid today. I especially appreciated his comment (page 3) on Sigmund Freud's theory that deep down inside we all really want to kill our fathers and sleep with our mothers! (Or, vice versa.)

Criminal law is very shallow. It does not examine the biological causes of crime or other scientific theories of guilt. In the 1760s, Sir William Blackstone said in his treatise *Commentaries on the Law of England* that "criminal responsibility is based upon that free will which God had given man." This doomed our criminal justice system. (It has failed.) I came away from these books and ideas with a new look at the system that was concerned with error on earth: punishing criminals—sociobiology.

The Whisperings Within is so powerful, I cannot analyze it. Every paragraph consumes me to this day. Starting with Darwin's theory of natural selection in *On the Origin of Species*, Barash awakened me to the education I missed as a child and young adult. When I first read this book, I was in my forties, learning how wrong my ideas were about human behavior. I didn't feel embarrassed; I felt tricked. My grandmother and my teachers had misled me. (I didn't know my mother, so Freud's theory above does not apply to my life. Or does it?) This book by Dr. Barash was as meaningful to me as Carl Sagan's *Dragons of Eden: Speculations on the Evolution of Human Intelligence*. I'll not try to review either of these books. I'll suggest you read both and draw your own conclusions. These books might alter your life as they have mine. These writers were critical thinkers.

In 1932, Edwin M. Borchard's *Convicting the Innocent* was published. I first obtained and read the book in the 1970s.

There have been many books and articles on the subject since then, especially since DNA has become a forensics tool that has exposed other terrible flaws in criminal justice. The system is not bulletproof. Innocent humans get convicted and are imprisoned. Some are executed. For this reason alone, the system is badly in need of repair or should be abolished. A system that allows erroneous criminal convictions is not acceptable. The 65 cases in Borchard's book are only a beginning. What's happened since then over the years is outrageous. The same errors continue today to be repeated over and over. My proposed solution is to abolish the system and start over.

As I see it, a billion years ago when sexual reproduction began, there was no "social" harm; there was no society. Later, "Caveman," any of the 20 or so species of our family discovered and identified so far, did not define crime. It was "survival of the fittest." Great apes and humans are both hominoids. Some scientists consider humans to be a species of ape. Of humans, only one species of human has survived. (Humans are genetically closer to chimpanzees. Chimpanzees are closer to humans than gorillas.) Our species invented crime, I suppose, to protect civilization from nature! Our cousins the other chimpanzees, the gorilla, the orangutan, obviously did not define crime or punish animal "criminals" as we do. It is peculiar to the surviving human species, *Homo sapiens*. (The law of the jungle has been replaced with religion.)

Why keep this system? Why not abolish prisons, courts, punishment, lawyers, judges, jurors, police, and identify the real cause of crime (biological) and cure it? Prevent crime. (Let God do the punishing.)

Genetic engineering is a solution. It's more than a matter of genes (DNA structures), as we now know. Epigenetics shows we inherit more than a DNA structure. In our 46 chromosomes and whatever else we inherit, is

138

material responsible for our behavior (I say 90 percent) and our life experiences or environment comprise the remainder. Attack these "causes," and crime could solve itself.

Recently I presented a two-hour PowerPoint slideshow and a paper entitled "Critical Thinking" to a civil rights class of law students at the University of St. Louis Law School, St. Louis, Missouri. It was a great learning experience for me. In the middle of my presentation, one of the students got up and disappeared. I wasn't shocked; I assumed I had offended her. I had a similar experience one other time in my life, when I was teaching criminal justice at the University of Memphis years ago. At age 79, I was used to cold reactions to my ideas. My ideas are different. My solution to crime is bold and unacceptable to most good citizens. I understand that.

My goal is to ask people to think—to question what we are doing with our religious system of justice for criminals, but I don't know exactly why the more recent student left. Did I say something specific that offended her? About 10 percent of my students, in my experience since 1990, come to class to argue or disagree with the teacher. Was she someone who came to class just to disagree, or was it deeper than that? I wish I knew. It would help me in rewriting my remarks and my PowerPoint.

I believe in love: kindness. I believe that the roots of good and evil are intertwined in each one of us. But the difference between love and hate or evil is narrow, hard to define, and there is a grey area. What really drives us in the unconscious to survive?

My dogs have taught me love. My dog Happy, a mountain cur, killed one of my baby chickens. I saw it in Happy's mouth. I watched and listened to the chick's mother (Egg Wolf) suffer. She had only two babies left. It was horrible. I was so depressed. I loved Happy. I loved the dead baby chick. I loved Egg Wolf. I love all ten of my chickens and the rooster, Thor. I also love all of my dogs: Happy, Missy (aka Mississippi), Waldo, and our latest, a Newfoundland/wolf puppy named Ladybug. Missy is a pit bull/mountain cur mix, and I saved her from death in a dog shelter near Mineral Wells, Texas, in 2015. Waldo we rescued also in Texas, in 2008. (Waldo is named for a deceased lawyer friend of my wife.)

I love these dogs.[29] I've had dogs all my life, but only recently have I learned about dog therapy, love, and kindness. Love is hard to define. You know love when you find love. It is love (kindness) that is the secret to curing crime. I'm sure. (What am I talking about?) The solution involves critical thinking and a different approach to crime. Punishment should be reserved for God's use.

My five-year-old grandson started kindergarten in Ohio in August 2015. He was with me for several summer months. I tried to get him ready for the shock of kindergarten. He needed lots of help. But I also learned from him. One morning I made some coffee and got him a glass of milk. I drank some of the coffee, and then I got a piece of cake. He looked at me and said, "What about me?" He got the cake.

One of my very best friends died suddenly at the age of 57. He had been suffering from an extremely high pulse rate, and the day before surgery to replace an upper heart valve, he suddenly died. His name was Kevin. Every day for over a year, at "Jack Daniels hour," I had crossed the highway to where Kevin was building his dream house for himself and his wife Pam, and we would have a drink or two and talk. When I left my house

---

29 There are about a billion dogs on Earth. About 750 million don't have flea collars. And they don't have humans who take them for walks and pick up their feces. They are called village dogs, street dogs, and free-breeding dogs, among other things, and they haunt the garbage dumps and neighborhoods of most of the world. This is extremely sad.

I would say to my wife, "I'm going over to Kevin's." My great-granddaughter, Marley, who was three, visited us often, and if she was here she would quickly say, "What about me?" I would, of course, take her with me, as she had learned to love Kevin also. It's that kind of love I'm talking about.

I look out over the mountains on my upper deck. I feel love (kindness) from some dogs, some chickens, two cats, a grandson, a great-granddaughter, and others, including Kevin. If society would approach crime with this kind of love (kindness) in its heart, I'm certain we'd find the solution to crime. It is survival of the fittest that drives us. We must forgive, not punish, those who trespass against us.

The purpose of this book is to cause the reader to think critically. One of my law graduate professors told me in the 1970s, "Become a problem solver." Carl Sagan introduced me to the idea of "critical thinking." Attack! Think! Be critical. Agree or disagree. Look for errors and omissions. What are your ideas for tomorrow? For the future? We are a DNA-driven software species. Environment is important, but I've changed my view from a 50-50 nature-nurture balance to 90-10. There may be some aspects of life that simply cannot be understood without understanding the mystery and majesty of the biological cell. Did I solve the problem? Perhaps we could start with a state or states for 40 years and keep detailed and accurate statistical records for the ultimate decision for all states. (The world?)

No one knows how a human decides to commit crime. A crime is any social harm defined and made punishable by law. So there were no crimes for millions of years, but primitive humans committed "criminal" acts with a "criminal" state of mind. (Was that evil?) It's in our genes and DNA, and life experiences shape us. If there is no free will, individuals are not to blame. Conviction and punishment are simply wrong.

What would primitive man (millions of years ago)—while building a fire with sticks of wood to cook—think, if you read to him about how a microwave oven works?

Dr. Irene Pepperbert (1949-), a Research Associate and lecturer at Harvard University, is the president and founder of the Alex Foundation, which she started for the purpose of supporting research that will expand the base of knowledge establishing the cognitive and communicative abilities of parrots as intelligent beings. In 1977, she purchased a year-old African gray parrot whom she named Alex. In their time together, Alex learned more than 100 words and differentiated between shapes and colors. He appeared to understand what he heard. Alex died in 2007. His last words to Irene were: "You be good. See you tomorrow. I love you."

Chimpanzees and some monkeys can beat college students on certain math problems. Some dolphins use shells to catch fish. Tiny zebra fish can also count. Chickadees look to the future. Bees learn from one another. Crickets weigh decisions. Black bears have demonstrated an ability to recognize pictures and understand abstract concepts. Much remains to be discovered.

The following quote is from Daniel C. Dennett's book, *Darwin's Dangerous Idea: Evolution and the Meanings of Life*:

> The Darwinian Revolution is both a scientific and a philosophical revolution, and neither revolution could have occurred without the other. As we shall see, it was the philosophical prejudices of the scientists, more than their lack of scientific evidence, that prevented them from seeing how the theory could actually work, but those philosophical prejudices that had to be overthrown were too deeply entrenched to be dislodged by mere philosophical brilliance. It took an irresistible parade of hard-won scientific facts to force thinkers

to take seriously the weird new outlook that Darwin proposed. Those who are still ill-acquainted with that beautiful procession can be forgiven their continued allegiance to the pre-Darwinian ideas. And the battle is not yet over; even among the scientists, there are pockets of resistance.

Let me lay my cards on the table. If I were to give an award for the single best idea anyone has ever had, I'd give it to Darwin, ahead of Newton and Einstein and everyone else. In a single stroke, the idea of evolution by natural selection unifies the realm of life, meaning, and purpose with the realm of space and time, cause and effect, mechanism and physical law. But it is not just a wonderful scientific idea. It is a dangerous idea. My admiration for Darwin's magnificent idea is unbounded, but I, too, cherish many of the ideas and ideals that it seems to challenge. (1995)

Darwin's idea is both the beginning and the end of understanding the cause of crime. We are animals. We are mammals. We evolved.

References

These are the sources that I am able to document. There may be others not mentioned here that were lost in my efforts to educate myself during my many-year quest. I apologize for any inadvertent omission of sources or information that may have resulted from incomplete notes. If you have any concerns about this, please email me at wittdaux@gmail.com. I will reply. I hope that this list of resources will inspire. I encourage all to help support these authors by purchasing and talking to others about those materials that spark interest.

Alex, B. (2016, December). Meet the Denisovans. *Discover Magazine*. Retrieved from http://discovermagazine.com/2016/dec/meet-the-denisovans

American incarceration. (2017). *Smithsonian Magazine*. Retrieved from https://www.smithsonianmag.com/history/far-reaching-effects-american-incarceration-180961435/

Barash, D. P. (1979). *The whisperings within: Evolution and the origin of human nature*. New York, NY: Harper & Row.

Bergland. R. (1989). *The fabric of mind*. London, England: Penguin Books.

Berra, T. M. (1990). *Evolution and the myth of creationism*. Redwood City, CA: Stanford University Press.

Blackmore, S. (2010). *Consciousness: An introduction*. (2nd Ed.). London, England: Routledge.

Blackstone, W. (2003). *Commentaries on the laws of England*. Clark, NJ: The Lawbook Exchange, Ltd. (Original work published 1765)

Borchard, E. M. (1982). *Convicting the innocent: Sixty-five actual errors of criminal justice*. New Haven, CT:

Yale University Press.

Bower, B. (2009, July 2). Neural feel for seeing: Emotion may mold early visual activity in brain. *Science News, 166*, 340–341.

Braverman, E. R. (2004). *The edge effect: Achieve total health and longevity with the balanced brain advantage.* New York, NY: Sterling Publishing.

Brockman, J. (Ed.). (2002). *The next fifty years: Science in the first half of the twenty-first century.* New York, NY: Random House, Inc.

Brodal, P. (1992). *The central nervous system: Structure and function.* New York, NY: Oxford University Press.

Bronowski, J. (1973). *The Ascent of Man.* New York, NY: Little, Brown & Co.

Bronowski, J. (Writer and Actor), & Malone, A. (Director). (1973). *The Ascent of Man*, Episode 12 [Motion Picture]. United States: BBC & Time-Life Films.

Brooks, D. (2011). *The social animal: The hidden sources of love, character, and achievement.* New York, NY: Random House, Inc.

Brown, M. H. (1990). *The search for Eve.* New York, NY: HarperCollins.

Brumfiel, G. (2014, March 20). Einstein's lost theory discovered...and it's wrong [Radio program]. *Morning Edition.* Washington, DC: NPR. Retrieved from https://www.npr.org/2014/03/20/291408248/einsteins-lost-theory-discovered-and-its-wrong

Brusatte, S., & Luo, Z. (2016, June). The ascent of mammals. *Scientific American, 314*, 28–35. Retrieved from www.thelukens.net/science/SciAmer/SciAm%20201606.pdf

Burgin, C. J., Colella, J. P., Kahn, P. L. & Upham, N. S. (2018, February 1). How many species of mammals are there? *Journal of Mammalogy, 99*(1), 1–14. Retrieved from https://doi.org/10.1093/jmammal/gyx147

Calaprice, A. (2005). *The New Quotable Einstein.* Princeton, NJ: Princeton University Press.

Challoner, J. (2015). *The cell: A visual tour of the building block of life.* Chicago, IL: University of Chicago Press.

Chambers, J., & Mitton, J. (2017). *From dust to life: The origin and evolution of our solar system.* Princeton, NJ: Princeton University Press.

Chandler, E. W. (1983, October 3). Genetic engineering: Will it be a viable solution to curb our nation's rising crime problem? *Memphis Press-Scimitar*, B1, B5.

Chandler, E. W. (1985, March 31). A criminal-free society through gene splicing. *The Commercial Appeal*, p. E3.

Chandler, E. W. (1985, November 13). Cloning criminals: The death of the doctrine of free will. Paper presented at the American Society of Criminology's 37th Annual Meeting, San Diego, California.

Chandler, E. W. (1998, June). Sex, death & lawyer's ethics. *ATLA Docket,* Arkansas Trial Lawyers Association, 12-18.

Chandler, E. W. (1999, Spring) The genetic defect defense. *ATLA Docket,* Arkansas Trial Lawyers Association, 8-13.

Coyne, J. A. (2010). *Why evolution is true.* New York, NY: Penguin Books.

Darrow, C. (1903). *Resist not evil.* Chicago, IL: Charles H. Kerr & Company.

Darwin, C. (2006). *On the origin of species by means of natural selection.* Mineola, NY: Dover Reprint. (Original work published 1859)

Darwin, C. (2004). *The descent of man and selection related to sex.* London, England: Penguin Classics Reprint. (Original work published 1871)

Davidson, R. J., Putnam, K. M., & Larson, C. L. (2000, July 28). Dysfunction in the neural circuitry of emotion regulation—A possible prelude to violence. *Science, 289*(5479), 591–594.

Davis, K. (2017). *The brain defense: Murder in Manhattan and the dawn of neuroscience in America's courtrooms.* New York, NY: Penguin Press.

Dennett, D. C. (1995). *Darwin's dangerous idea: Evolution and the meanings of life.* New York, NY: Simon & Schuster Inc.

Diamond, J. (1992). *The third chimpanzee: The evolution and future of the human animal.* New York, NY: HarperCollins Publishers, Inc.

Discovery of new Tiktaalik roseae fossils reveals key link in evolution of hind limbs. (2014). University of Chicago Medical Center. *EurekAlert!* American Association for the Advancement of Science. Retrieved from https://www.eurekalert.org/pub_releases/2014-01/uocm-don010714.php

Enserink, M. (2000, July 28). Searching for the mark of Cain. *Science, 575*–579.

Fields, R. D. (2009). *The other brain: From dementia to schizophrenia.* New York, NY: Simon & Schuster, Inc.

Fine, C. (2008). *The Britannica guide to the brain.* London, England: Constable & Robinson Ltd.

Folger, T. (2014, July 14). Journeys to the center of the Earth: Our planet's core powers a magnetic field that shields us from a hostile cosmos. But how does it really work? *Discover Magazine*. Retrieved from http://discovermagazine.com/2014/julyaug/13-journeys-to-the-center-of-the-earth

Fox, D. (2019, January 3). Space rocks are revealing the history of our solar system. *Discover Magazine*. Retrieved from http://discovermagazine.com/2017/june/our-rocks-ourselves

Francis, R. C. (2011). *Epigenetics: How environment shapes our genes*. New York, NY: W. W. Norton & Company, Inc.

Friel, J. C., & Friel, L. D. (2012). *The power and grace between nasty or nice: Replacing entitlement, narcissism, and incivility with knowledge, caring, and genuine self-esteem*. Deerfield Beach, FL: HCI Books.

Fymat, A. L. (2017). Genetics, epigenetics and cancer. *Cancer Therapy & Oncology International Journal, 4*(2). doi: 10.19080/CTOIJ.2017.04.555634

Gannon, M. (2016, January 8). Fireball down under: Researchers uncover older-than-Earth meteorite. *Live Science*. Retrieved from https://www.livescience.com/53310-fireball-meteorite-discovered-australia-outback.html

Gee, H. (2015). *The accidental species: Misunderstandings of human evolution*. Chicago, IL: University of Chicago Press.

Gleiser, M. (2013, September 25). Lessons from the heliosphere [Radio program]. Washington, DC: NPR. Retrieved from https://www.npr.org/sections/13.7/2013/09/24/225807337/lessons-from-beyond-the-heliopause

Goldman, D. (1996, November 29). High anxiety. *Science, 274*(5292), 1483.

Greene, G. L., & Geltenbort, P. (2016, April). The neutron enigma. *Scientific American, 314*(4), 37–41. Retrieved from https://pdfs.semanticscholar.org/ dc98/84b77202021959e458b7e71b461572edb0bd.pdf

Gurney, J. (2016). Dino for dinner. [Oil painting]. In S. Brusatte and Z. Luo. The ascent of mammals. *Scientific American, 314,* 29. Retrieved from www. thelukens.net/science/SciAmer/SciAm%20201606. pdf

Harsanyi, Z., & Hutton, R. (1981). *Genetic prophecy: Beyond the double helix*. New York, NY: Rawson, Wade Publishers.

Hart, C. (2008). *Secrets of serotonin: The natural hormone that curbs food and alcohol cravings, reduces pain, and elevates your mood*. New York, NY: St. Martin's Press.

Jastrow, R. (1977). *Until the sun dies*. New York, NY: W. W. Norton & Co.

Johanson, D. C., & Edey, M. (1981). *Lucy: The beginnings of humankind*. New York, NY: Simon & Schuster, Inc.

Kingsley, R. E. (1996). *Concise text of neuroscience*. Philadelphia, PA: Williams & Wilkins.

Klebanow, D., & Jonas, F. L. (2003). People's lawyers: Crusaders for justice in American history. Armonk, NY: M. E. Sharpe.

Kotulak, R. (1993, December 13). How brain's chemistry unleashes violence. *Chicago Tribune*. Retrieved from https://www.chicagotribune.com/news/ct-xpm-1993-12-13-9312130209-story.html

Kotulak, R. (1997). *Inside the brain: Revolutionary discoveries of how the mind works*. Kansas City, MO: Andrews McMeel Publishing.

Küppers, B. O. (1989). *Information and the origin of life*. Cambridge, MA: MIT Press.

Lawrence, J., & Lee, R. E. (2003). *Inherit the wind*. New York, NY: Ballantine Books Reprint. (Original play performed 1955)

Leakey, R. E., & Lewin, R. (1977). *Origins: The emergence and evolution of our species and its possible future*. New York, NY: E. P. Dutton Publishers.

LeDoux, J. (2002). *Synaptic self: How our brains become who we are*. New York, NY: Penguin Putnam, Inc.

Lee, J. J. (2013). 6 women scientists who were snubbed due to sexism. *National Geographic Daily News*. Retrieved from https://news.nationalgeographic.com/news/2013/13/130519-women-scientists-overlooked-dna-history-science/

Leeming, D. A. (1990). *The world of myth*. New York, NY: Oxford University Press.

Lewis, T. (2013, October 2). Polar opposites: Why climate change affects Arctic & Antarctic differently. *LiveScience*. Retrieved from https://www.livescience.com/40125-climate-change-affecting-arctic-antarctic-differently.html

Livio, M. (2013). *Brilliant blunders: From Darwin to Einstein—colossal mistakes by great scientists that changed our understanding of life and the universe*. New York, NY: Simon & Schuster.

LSST General Public FAQs. (2018). LSST: The large synoptic survey telescope. Retrieved from https://www.lsst.org/content/lsst-general-public-faqs

Lynch, G., & Granger, R. (2008). *Big brain: The origins and future of human intelligence*. New York, NY: St. Martin's Press LLC.

Machiavelli, N. (1995). *The Prince. (*Ninian Hill Thompson, Trans.). Oxford, England: Clarendon Press. (Original work published 1532)

Mani, S. K., Allen, J. M., Clark, J. H., Blaustein, J. D., & O'Malley, B. W. (1994, August 26). Convergent pathways for steroid hormone- and neurotransmitter-induced rat sexual behavior. *Science, 265*(5176), 1246–1249.

Manning, C. (2012, November 15). Farish Jenkins, Jr., 72. The Harvard Gazette. Retrieved from https://news.harvard.edu/gazette/story/2012/11/farish-a-jenkins-jr-72/

Marsa, L. (2009, February 10). Six sites that are the Galapagos for modern Darwins: Researchers see amazing twists of evolution at the biological hot spots. *Discover Magazine.* Retrieved from http://discovermagazine.com/2009/mar/10-six-sites-that-are-the-galapagos-for-modern-darwins

McGowan, K. (Ed.). (2011). Evolution: Rethinking the story of life [Special issue]. *Discover Magazine.*

McGowan, K. (2014). How life made the leap from single cells to multicellular animals. Retrieved from https://www.wired.com/2014/08/where-animals-come-from/

Menninger, K. (1968). *The crime of punishment.* Bloomington, IN: AuthorHouse.

New CASA report finds: 65% of all U.S. inmates meet medical criteria for substance abuse addiction. (2010, February 26). Center on Addiction. Retrieved from https://www.centeronaddiction.org/newsroom/press-releases/2010-behind-bars-II

Niehoff, D. (1999). *The biology of violence.* New York, NY: Simon & Schuster, Inc.

Olson, S. (2003). *Mapping human history: Genes, race, and our common origins.* Boston, MA: Mariner Books.

Oppenheimer, S. (2003). *The real Eve: Modern man's journey out of Africa.* New York, NY: Carroll & Graf Publishers.

Pallen, M. (2009). *The rough guide to evolution: Darwin's big idea that changed the world.* London, England: Penguin Books.

Pert, C. B. (1997). *Molecules of emotion: Why you feel the way you feel.* New York, NY: Simon & Schuster, Inc.

Physics at the limits. (2015, December). Special Collector's Edition. *Scientific American,* 24(4s).

Powell, C. S. (2014, March 19). Rumblings from the massive black hole at the center of our galaxy. *Discover Magazine.* Retrieved from http://discovermagazine.com/2014/april/15-when-a-slumbering-monster-awakens

Powell, C. S. (2016, October). To Planet 9—And beyond! *Discover Magazine.* Retrieved from http://discovermagazine.com/2016/oct/to-planet-9

Public's views on human evolution. (2013). Pew Research Center: Religion and Public Life. Retrieved from http://www.pewforum.org/2013/12/30/publics-views-on-human-evolution/

Pyne, L. (2016). *Seven skeletons: The evolution of the world's most famous human fossils.* Austin, TX: University of Texas.

Raine, A. (2013). *The anatomy of violence: The biological roots of crime.* New York, NY: Random House, Inc.

Rendsburg, G. A. (2006). *The book of genesis*. The Great Courses. Chantilly, VA: The Teaching Company.

Richter, V. (n.d.). The five big mass extinctions. *Cosmos: The Science of Everything*. Retrieved from https://cosmosmagazine.com/palaeontology/big-five-extinctions

Sagan, C. (1977). *Dragons of Eden: Speculations on the evolution of human intelligence*. New York, NY: The Random House Publishing Group.

Sapolsky, R. (2003, September). Taming stress. *Scientific American, 289*(3), 87–95.

Sapolsky, R. (2005). *Biology and human behavior: The neurological origins of individuality*. Chantilly, VA: The Teaching Company.

Sapolsky, R. M. (2007). *Behave: The biology of humans at our best and worst*. New York, NY: Penguin Press.

Saudou, F., Amara, D. A., Dierich, A., LeMeur, M., Ramboz, S., Segu, L.,...Hen, R. (1994, September 23). Enhanced aggressive behavior in mice lacking 5-HT1B receptor. *Science, 265*(5180), 1875–1878.

Selim, J. (2002, December). The gene of all fears. *Discover Magazine*, 14.

Shengold, L. (1989). *Soul murder: The effects of childhood abuse and deprivation*. New Haven, CT: Yale University Press.

Shermer, M. (2006, October 1). Darwin on the right: Why Christians and conservatives should accept evolution. *Scientific American*. Retrieved from https://www.scientificamerican.com/article/darwin-on-the-right/

Shubin, N. (2009). *Your inner fish: A journey into the 3.5-billion-year history of the human body*. New York, NY: Random House.

Spencer, H. (1864). *Principles of biology*. Covent Garden, London: Williams and Norgate.

Spencer, G. (2005). New genome comparison finds chimps, humans very similar at the DNA level. *NIH News*, National Human Genome Research Institute. Retrieved from https://www.genome. gov/15515096/2005-release-new-genome-comparison-finds-chimps-humans-very-similar-at-dna-level/

Strauss, M. (2015, September 12). 12 theories of how we became human, and why they're all wrong. *National Geographic*. Retrieved from https://news. nationalgeographic.com/2015/09/150911-how-we-became-human-theories-evolution-science/

Stringer, C. (2012). *Lone survivors: How we came to be the only humans on earth*. New York, NY: Henry Holt and Company, LLC.

Tarlach, G. (2015, November 25). 20 things you didn't know about lava: Did lava kill the dinosaurs? Maybe. *Discover Magazine*. Retrieved from http://discovermagazine.com/2015/dec/20-20-things-you-didnt-know-about-lava

Tegmark, M. (2003, May). Parallel universes. *Scientific American,* 41-51. https://space.mit.edu/home/tegmark/PDF/multiverse_sciam.pdf

Tierney, J., Wright, L., & Springer, K. (1988, January 11). The search for Adam and Eve. *Newsweek*, 46–52.

Tierney, J. (2017, June 9). The tyranny of the administrative state. *Wall Street Journal*. Retrieved from https://www.wsj.com/articles/the-tyranny-of-the-administrative-state-1497037492

Tudge, C. (1999). *Neanderthals, bandits and farmers: How agriculture really began*. New Haven, CT: Yale

University Press.

Ungar, P. S. (2017). *Evolution's bite: A story of teeth, diet, and human origins.* Princeton, NJ: Princeton University Press.

Wallace, A. R. (2009). On the law which has regulated the introduction of new species. *Alfred Russel Wallace Classic Writings.* Paper 2. (Original work published 1885.) Retrieved from https://digitalcommons.wku.edu/dlps_fac_arw/2

Walter, W. J. (2013). *Last ape standing: The seven-million-year story of how and why we survived.* New York, NY: Walker Publishing Company, Inc.

Weinberg, A. (Ed.). (1957). *Attorney for the damned: Clarence Darrow in the courtroom.* Chicago, IL: University of Chicago Press.

Weinberg, S. (1977). *The first three minutes: A modern view of the origin of the universe.* New York, NY: BasicBooks.

Wells, S. (2003). *The journey of man: A genetic odyssey.* Princeton, NY: Princeton University Press.

What does it mean to be human? Homo naledi. (2018). Smithsonian Museum of Natural History: Human Evolution Evidence. Retrieved from http://humanorigins.si.edu/evidence/human-fossils/species/homo-naledi

Wilson, E. O. (1975). *Sociobiology: The new synthesis.* Cambridge, MA: The Belknap Press of Harvard University Press.

Wong, K. (2012, April). First of our kind: Could Australopithecus sediba be our long lost ancestor? *Scientific American.* Retrieved from https://www.scientificamerican.com/article/first-of-our-kind/

Wong, K. (2017, May 10). New evidence of mysterious homo naledi raises questions about how humans evolved. *Scientific American*. Retrieved from https://www.scientificamerican.com/article/new-evidence-of-mysterious-homo-naledi-raises-questions-about-how-humans-evolved/

World population. (2019). Worldometers. Retrieved from http://www.worldometers.info/world-population/

Your cells—living libraries! (2019). Retrieved from https://www.jw.org/en/publications/magazines/g201508/dna-in-your-cells/

Zeman, A. (2009). *A portrait of the brain*. New Haven, CT: Yale University Press.

Zimmer, C. (2005). *Smithsonian intimate guide to human origins*. Washington, DC: Smithsonian Books.

Zimmer, C. (2014, March). The oldest rocks on Earth. *Scientific American*. 59–63. Retrieved from https://justin.vashonsd.org/projects/rock/scientificamerican0314-58-4.4byoGreenstone.pdf

Zorich, Z. (2016, July/August). Tracking when humans, Neanderthals, and Denisovans crossed paths—and what became of their offspring. *Archaeology Magazine*. Retrieved from https://www.magzter.com/articles/3357/168462/57e0d8cf6b6cf